C-4718 CAREER EXAMINATION SERIES

This is your
PASSBOOK for...

Emergency Medical Services (EMS) Coordinator

Test Preparation Study Guide
Questions & Answers

NATIONAL LEARNING CORPORATION®

COPYRIGHT NOTICE

This book is SOLELY intended for, is sold ONLY to, and its use is RESTRICTED to individual, bona fide applicants or candidates who qualify by virtue of having seriously filed applications for appropriate license, certificate, professional and/or promotional advancement, higher school matriculation, scholarship, or other legitimate requirements of education and/or governmental authorities.

This book is NOT intended for use, class instruction, tutoring, training, duplication, copying, reprinting, excerption, or adaptation, etc., by:

1) Other publishers
2) Proprietors and/or Instructors of "Coaching" and/or Preparatory Courses
3) Personnel and/or Training Divisions of commercial, industrial, and governmental organizations
4) Schools, colleges, or universities and/or their departments and staffs, including teachers and other personnel
5) Testing Agencies or Bureaus
6) Study groups which seek by the purchase of a single volume to copy and/or duplicate and/or adapt this material for use by the group as a whole without having purchased individual volumes for each of the members of the group
7) Et al.

Such persons would be in violation of appropriate Federal and State statutes.

PROVISION OF LICENSING AGREEMENTS – Recognized educational, commercial, industrial, and governmental institutions and organizations, and others legitimately engaged in educational pursuits, including training, testing, and measurement activities, may address request for a licensing agreement to the copyright owners, who will determine whether, and under what conditions, including fees and charges, the materials in this book may be used them. In other words, a licensing facility exists for the legitimate use of the material in this book on other than an individual basis. However, it is asseverated and affirmed here that the material in this book CANNOT be used without the receipt of the express permission of such a licensing agreement from the Publishers. Inquiries re licensing should be addressed to the company, attention rights and permissions department.

All rights reserved, including the right of reproduction in whole or in part, in any form or by any means, electronic or mechanical, including photocopying, recording, or by any information storage and retrieval system, without permission in writing from the Publisher.

Copyright © 2024 by
National Learning Corporation

212 Michael Drive, Syosset, NY 11791
(516) 921-8888 • www.passbooks.com
E-mail: info@passbooks.com

PUBLISHED IN THE UNITED STATES OF AMERICA

PASSBOOK® SERIES

THE *PASSBOOK® SERIES* has been created to prepare applicants and candidates for the ultimate academic battlefield – the examination room.

At some time in our lives, each and every one of us may be required to take an examination – for validation, matriculation, admission, qualification, registration, certification, or licensure.

Based on the assumption that every applicant or candidate has met the basic formal educational standards, has taken the required number of courses, and read the necessary texts, the *PASSBOOK® SERIES* furnishes the one special preparation which may assure passing with confidence, instead of failing with insecurity. Examination questions – together with answers – are furnished as the basic vehicle for study so that the mysteries of the examination and its compounding difficulties may be eliminated or diminished by a sure method.

This book is meant to help you pass your examination provided that you qualify and are serious in your objective.

The entire field is reviewed through the huge store of content information which is succinctly presented through a provocative and challenging approach – the question-and-answer method.

A climate of success is established by furnishing the correct answers at the end of each test.

You soon learn to recognize types of questions, forms of questions, and patterns of questioning. You may even begin to anticipate expected outcomes.

You perceive that many questions are repeated or adapted so that you can gain acute insights, which may enable you to score many sure points.

You learn how to confront new questions, or types of questions, and to attack them confidently and work out the correct answers.

You note objectives and emphases, and recognize pitfalls and dangers, so that you may make positive educational adjustments.

Moreover, you are kept fully informed in relation to new concepts, methods, practices, and directions in the field.

You discover that you are actually taking the examination all the time: you are preparing for the examination by "taking" an examination, not by reading extraneous and/or supererogatory textbooks.

In short, this PASSBOOK®, used directedly, should be an important factor in helping you to pass your test.

EMERGENCY MEDICAL SERVICES (EMS) COORDINATOR

DUTIES:
The work involves responsibility for coordinating the delivery of emergency medical support services among the various ambulance/emergency medical service providers. The incumbent is responsible for coordinating a comprehensive response to major emergencies/disasters involving mass/multiple casualties. The incumbent identifies and works with private, public, and voluntary emergency medical service providers in the preparation of emergency plans and the coordination of field training programs for emergency personnel. The work is performed under the general supervision of the Emergency Services Director with considerable leeway allowed for the exercise of independent judgement in carrying out details of the work. The incumbent does related work as required.

SCOPE OF THE EXAMINATION:
The written test will cover knowledge, skills and/or abilities in such areas as:

1. **Ensuring effective inter/intra agency communications** - These questions test for understanding of techniques for interacting effectively with individuals and agencies, to educate and inform them about topics of concern, to clarify agency programs or policies, to negotiate conflicts or resolve complaints, and to represent one's agency or program in a manner in keeping with good public relations practices. Questions may also cover interacting with the staff of one's own agency and/or that of other agencies in cooperative efforts of public outreach or service.
2. **Preparing written material** - These questions test for the ability to present information clearly and accurately, and to organize paragraphs logically and comprehensibly. For some questions, you will be given information in two or three sentences followed by four restatements of the information. You must then choose the best version. For other questions, you will be given paragraphs with their sentences out of order. You must then choose, from four suggestions, the best order for the sentences.
3. **Principles and practices of staff development and training** - These questions test for the knowledge and abilities used to develop and deliver training. They address topics such as the assessment of training needs; instructional design, training methods and techniques; the use of training aids, materials, and technology; motivation; learning theory; classroom management; the evaluation of learning outcomes; and the usage of training-related data.
4. **Program planning and evaluation** - These questions test for a knowledge of basic concepts and techniques in such areas as the planning function, factors involved in implementing new procedures or programs, and evaluating their results and effectiveness. The questions are conceptual in approach and fundamental in level; they do not involve the manipulation of data nor the application of quantitative methods.
5. **Understanding and interpreting written material** - These questions test how well you comprehend written material. You will be provided with brief reading selections and will be asked questions about the selections. All the information required to answer the questions will be presented in the selections; you will not be required to have any special knowledge relating to the subject areas of the selections.

HOW TO TAKE A TEST

I. YOU MUST PASS AN EXAMINATION

A. *WHAT EVERY CANDIDATE SHOULD KNOW*

Examination applicants often ask us for help in preparing for the written test. What can I study in advance? What kinds of questions will be asked? How will the test be given? How will the papers be graded?

As an applicant for a civil service examination, you may be wondering about some of these things. Our purpose here is to suggest effective methods of advance study and to describe civil service examinations.

Your chances for success on this examination can be increased if you know how to prepare. Those "pre-examination jitters" can be reduced if you know what to expect. You can even experience an adventure in good citizenship if you know why civil service exams are given.

B. *WHY ARE CIVIL SERVICE EXAMINATIONS GIVEN?*

Civil service examinations are important to you in two ways. As a citizen, you want public jobs filled by employees who know how to do their work. As a job seeker, you want a fair chance to compete for that job on an equal footing with other candidates. The best-known means of accomplishing this two-fold goal is the competitive examination.

Exams are widely publicized throughout the nation. They may be administered for jobs in federal, state, city, municipal, town or village governments or agencies.

Any citizen may apply, with some limitations, such as the age or residence of applicants. Your experience and education may be reviewed to see whether you meet the requirements for the particular examination. When these requirements exist, they are reasonable and applied consistently to all applicants. Thus, a competitive examination may cause you some uneasiness now, but it is your privilege and safeguard.

C. *HOW ARE CIVIL SERVICE EXAMS DEVELOPED?*

Examinations are carefully written by trained technicians who are specialists in the field known as "psychological measurement," in consultation with recognized authorities in the field of work that the test will cover. These experts recommend the subject matter areas or skills to be tested; only those knowledges or skills important to your success on the job are included. The most reliable books and source materials available are used as references. Together, the experts and technicians judge the difficulty level of the questions.

Test technicians know how to phrase questions so that the problem is clearly stated. Their ethics do not permit "trick" or "catch" questions. Questions may have been tried out on sample groups, or subjected to statistical analysis, to determine their usefulness.

Written tests are often used in combination with performance tests, ratings of training and experience, and oral interviews. All of these measures combine to form the best-known means of finding the right person for the right job.

II. HOW TO PASS THE WRITTEN TEST

A. NATURE OF THE EXAMINATION

To prepare intelligently for civil service examinations, you should know how they differ from school examinations you have taken. In school you were assigned certain definite pages to read or subjects to cover. The examination questions were quite detailed and usually emphasized memory. Civil service exams, on the other hand, try to discover your present ability to perform the duties of a position, plus your potentiality to learn these duties. In other words, a civil service exam attempts to predict how successful you will be. Questions cover such a broad area that they cannot be as minute and detailed as school exam questions.

In the public service similar kinds of work, or positions, are grouped together in one "class." This process is known as *position-classification*. All the positions in a class are paid according to the salary range for that class. One class title covers all of these positions, and they are all tested by the same examination.

B. FOUR BASIC STEPS

1) Study the announcement

How, then, can you know what subjects to study? Our best answer is: "Learn as much as possible about the class of positions for which you've applied." The exam will test the knowledge, skills and abilities needed to do the work.

Your most valuable source of information about the position you want is the official exam announcement. This announcement lists the training and experience qualifications. Check these standards and apply only if you come reasonably close to meeting them.

The brief description of the position in the examination announcement offers some clues to the subjects which will be tested. Think about the job itself. Review the duties in your mind. Can you perform them, or are there some in which you are rusty? Fill in the blank spots in your preparation.

Many jurisdictions preview the written test in the exam announcement by including a section called "Knowledge and Abilities Required," "Scope of the Examination," or some similar heading. Here you will find out specifically what fields will be tested.

2) Review your own background

Once you learn in general what the position is all about, and what you need to know to do the work, ask yourself which subjects you already know fairly well and which need improvement. You may wonder whether to concentrate on improving your strong areas or on building some background in your fields of weakness. When the announcement has specified "some knowledge" or "considerable knowledge," or has used adjectives like "beginning principles of…" or "advanced … methods," you can get a clue as to the number and difficulty of questions to be asked in any given field. More questions, and hence broader coverage, would be included for those subjects which are more important in the work. Now weigh your strengths and weaknesses against the job requirements and prepare accordingly.

3) Determine the level of the position

Another way to tell how intensively you should prepare is to understand the level of the job for which you are applying. Is it the entering level? In other words, is this the position in which beginners in a field of work are hired? Or is it an intermediate or advanced level? Sometimes this is indicated by such words as "Junior" or "Senior" in the class title. Other jurisdictions use Roman numerals to designate the level – Clerk I, Clerk II, for example. The word "Supervisor" sometimes appears in the title. If the level is not indicated by the title, check the description of duties. Will you be working under very close supervision, or will you have responsibility for independent decisions in this work?

4) Choose appropriate study materials

Now that you know the subjects to be examined and the relative amount of each subject to be covered, you can choose suitable study materials. For beginning level jobs, or even advanced ones, if you have a pronounced weakness in some aspect of your training, read a modern, standard textbook in that field. Be sure it is up to date and has general coverage. Such books are normally available at your library, and the librarian will be glad to help you locate one. For entry-level positions, questions of appropriate difficulty are chosen – neither highly advanced questions, nor those too simple. Such questions require careful thought but not advanced training.

If the position for which you are applying is technical or advanced, you will read more advanced, specialized material. If you are already familiar with the basic principles of your field, elementary textbooks would waste your time. Concentrate on advanced textbooks and technical periodicals. Think through the concepts and review difficult problems in your field.

These are all general sources. You can get more ideas on your own initiative, following these leads. For example, training manuals and publications of the government agency which employs workers in your field can be useful, particularly for technical and professional positions. A letter or visit to the government department involved may result in more specific study suggestions, and certainly will provide you with a more definite idea of the exact nature of the position you are seeking.

III. KINDS OF TESTS

Tests are used for purposes other than measuring knowledge and ability to perform specified duties. For some positions, it is equally important to test ability to make adjustments to new situations or to profit from training. In others, basic mental abilities not dependent on information are essential. Questions which test these things may not appear as pertinent to the duties of the position as those which test for knowledge and information. Yet they are often highly important parts of a fair examination. For very general questions, it is almost impossible to help you direct your study efforts. What we can do is to point out some of the more common of these general abilities needed in public service positions and describe some typical questions.

1) General information

Broad, general information has been found useful for predicting job success in some kinds of work. This is tested in a variety of ways, from vocabulary lists to questions about current events. Basic background in some field of work, such as sociology or economics, may be sampled in a group of questions. Often these are principles which have become familiar to most persons through exposure rather than through formal training. It is difficult to advise you how to study for these questions; being alert to the world around you is our best suggestion.

2) Verbal ability

An example of an ability needed in many positions is verbal or language ability. Verbal ability is, in brief, the ability to use and understand words. Vocabulary and grammar tests are typical measures of this ability. Reading comprehension or paragraph interpretation questions are common in many kinds of civil service tests. You are given a paragraph of written material and asked to find its central meaning.

3) Numerical ability

Number skills can be tested by the familiar arithmetic problem, by checking paired lists of numbers to see which are alike and which are different, or by interpreting charts and graphs. In the latter test, a graph may be printed in the test booklet which you are asked to use as the basis for answering questions.

4) Observation

A popular test for law-enforcement positions is the observation test. A picture is shown to you for several minutes, then taken away. Questions about the picture test your ability to observe both details and larger elements.

5) Following directions

In many positions in the public service, the employee must be able to carry out written instructions dependably and accurately. You may be given a chart with several columns, each column listing a variety of information. The questions require you to carry out directions involving the information given in the chart.

6) Skills and aptitudes

Performance tests effectively measure some manual skills and aptitudes. When the skill is one in which you are trained, such as typing or shorthand, you can practice. These tests are often very much like those given in business school or high school courses. For many of the other skills and aptitudes, however, no short-time preparation can be made. Skills and abilities natural to you or that you have developed throughout your lifetime are being tested.

Many of the general questions just described provide all the data needed to answer the questions and ask you to use your reasoning ability to find the answers. Your best preparation for these tests, as well as for tests of facts and ideas, is to be at your physical and mental best. You, no doubt, have your own methods of getting into an exam-taking mood and keeping "in shape." The next section lists some ideas on this subject.

IV. KINDS OF QUESTIONS

Only rarely is the "essay" question, which you answer in narrative form, used in civil service tests. Civil service tests are usually of the short-answer type. Full instructions for answering these questions will be given to you at the examination. But in case this is your first experience with short-answer questions and separate answer sheets, here is what you need to know:

1) Multiple-choice Questions

Most popular of the short-answer questions is the "multiple choice" or "best answer" question. It can be used, for example, to test for factual knowledge, ability to solve problems or judgment in meeting situations found at work.

A multiple-choice question is normally one of three types—
- It can begin with an incomplete statement followed by several possible endings. You are to find the one ending which *best* completes the statement, although some of the others may not be entirely wrong.
- It can also be a complete statement in the form of a question which is answered by choosing one of the statements listed.

- It can be in the form of a problem – again you select the best answer.

Here is an example of a multiple-choice question with a discussion which should give you some clues as to the method for choosing the right answer:

When an employee has a complaint about his assignment, the action which will *best* help him overcome his difficulty is to
- A. discuss his difficulty with his coworkers
- B. take the problem to the head of the organization
- C. take the problem to the person who gave him the assignment
- D. say nothing to anyone about his complaint

In answering this question, you should study each of the choices to find which is best. Consider choice "A" – Certainly an employee may discuss his complaint with fellow employees, but no change or improvement can result, and the complaint remains unresolved. Choice "B" is a poor choice since the head of the organization probably does not know what assignment you have been given, and taking your problem to him is known as "going over the head" of the supervisor. The supervisor, or person who made the assignment, is the person who can clarify it or correct any injustice. Choice "C" is, therefore, correct. To say nothing, as in choice "D," is unwise. Supervisors have and interest in knowing the problems employees are facing, and the employee is seeking a solution to his problem.

2) True/False Questions

The "true/false" or "right/wrong" form of question is sometimes used. Here a complete statement is given. Your job is to decide whether the statement is right or wrong.

SAMPLE: A roaming cell-phone call to a nearby city costs less than a non-roaming call to a distant city.

This statement is wrong, or false, since roaming calls are more expensive.

This is not a complete list of all possible question forms, although most of the others are variations of these common types. You will always get complete directions for answering questions. Be sure you understand *how* to mark your answers – ask questions until you do.

V. RECORDING YOUR ANSWERS

Computer terminals are used more and more today for many different kinds of exams.

For an examination with very few applicants, you may be told to record your answers in the test booklet itself. Separate answer sheets are much more common. If this separate answer sheet is to be scored by machine – and this is often the case – it is highly important that you mark your answers correctly in order to get credit.

An electronic scoring machine is often used in civil service offices because of the speed with which papers can be scored. Machine-scored answer sheets must be marked with a pencil, which will be given to you. This pencil has a high graphite content which responds to the electronic scoring machine. As a matter of fact, stray dots may register as answers, so do not let your pencil rest on the answer sheet while you are pondering the correct answer. Also, if your pencil lead breaks or is otherwise defective, ask for another.

Since the answer sheet will be dropped in a slot in the scoring machine, be careful not to bend the corners or get the paper crumpled.

The answer sheet normally has five vertical columns of numbers, with 30 numbers to a column. These numbers correspond to the question numbers in your test booklet. After each number, going across the page are four or five pairs of dotted lines. These short dotted lines have small letters or numbers above them. The first two pairs may also have a "T" or "F" above the letters. This indicates that the first two pairs only are to be used if the questions are of the true-false type. If the questions are multiple choice, disregard the "T" and "F" and pay attention only to the small letters or numbers.

Answer your questions in the manner of the sample that follows:

32. The largest city in the United States is
    A. Washington, D.C.
    B. New York City
    C. Chicago
    D. Detroit
    E. San Francisco

1) Choose the answer you think is best. (New York City is the largest, so "B" is correct.)
2) Find the row of dotted lines numbered the same as the question you are answering. (Find row number 32)
3) Find the pair of dotted lines corresponding to the answer. (Find the pair of lines under the mark "B.")
4) Make a solid black mark between the dotted lines.

VI. BEFORE THE TEST

Common sense will help you find procedures to follow to get ready for an examination. Too many of us, however, overlook these sensible measures. Indeed, nervousness and fatigue have been found to be the most serious reasons why applicants fail to do their best on civil service tests. Here is a list of reminders:

- Begin your preparation early – Don't wait until the last minute to go scurrying around for books and materials or to find out what the position is all about.
- Prepare continuously – An hour a night for a week is better than an all-night cram session. This has been definitely established. What is more, a night a week for a month will return better dividends than crowding your study into a shorter period of time.
- Locate the place of the exam – You have been sent a notice telling you when and where to report for the examination. If the location is in a different town or otherwise unfamiliar to you, it would be well to inquire the best route and learn something about the building.
- Relax the night before the test – Allow your mind to rest. Do not study at all that night. Plan some mild recreation or diversion; then go to bed early and get a good night's sleep.
- Get up early enough to make a leisurely trip to the place for the test – This way unforeseen events, traffic snarls, unfamiliar buildings, etc. will not upset you.
- Dress comfortably – A written test is not a fashion show. You will be known by number and not by name, so wear something comfortable.

- Leave excess paraphernalia at home – Shopping bags and odd bundles will get in your way. You need bring only the items mentioned in the official notice you received; usually everything you need is provided. Do not bring reference books to the exam. They will only confuse those last minutes and be taken away from you when in the test room.
- Arrive somewhat ahead of time – If because of transportation schedules you must get there very early, bring a newspaper or magazine to take your mind off yourself while waiting.
- Locate the examination room – When you have found the proper room, you will be directed to the seat or part of the room where you will sit. Sometimes you are given a sheet of instructions to read while you are waiting. Do not fill out any forms until you are told to do so; just read them and be prepared.
- Relax and prepare to listen to the instructions
- If you have any physical problem that may keep you from doing your best, be sure to tell the test administrator. If you are sick or in poor health, you really cannot do your best on the exam. You can come back and take the test some other time.

VII. AT THE TEST

The day of the test is here and you have the test booklet in your hand. The temptation to get going is very strong. Caution! There is more to success than knowing the right answers. You must know how to identify your papers and understand variations in the type of short-answer question used in this particular examination. Follow these suggestions for maximum results from your efforts:

1) Cooperate with the monitor

The test administrator has a duty to create a situation in which you can be as much at ease as possible. He will give instructions, tell you when to begin, check to see that you are marking your answer sheet correctly, and so on. He is not there to guard you, although he will see that your competitors do not take unfair advantage. He wants to help you do your best.

2) Listen to all instructions

Don't jump the gun! Wait until you understand all directions. In most civil service tests you get more time than you need to answer the questions. So don't be in a hurry. Read each word of instructions until you clearly understand the meaning. Study the examples, listen to all announcements and follow directions. Ask questions if you do not understand what to do.

3) Identify your papers

Civil service exams are usually identified by number only. You will be assigned a number; you must not put your name on your test papers. Be sure to copy your number correctly. Since more than one exam may be given, copy your exact examination title.

4) Plan your time

Unless you are told that a test is a "speed" or "rate of work" test, speed itself is usually not important. Time enough to answer all the questions will be provided, but this does not mean that you have all day. An overall time limit has been set. Divide the total time (in minutes) by the number of questions to determine the approximate time you have for each question.

5) Do not linger over difficult questions

If you come across a difficult question, mark it with a paper clip (useful to have along) and come back to it when you have been through the booklet. One caution if you do this – be sure to skip a number on your answer sheet as well. Check often to be sure that you have not lost your place and that you are marking in the row numbered the same as the question you are answering.

6) Read the questions

Be sure you know what the question asks! Many capable people are unsuccessful because they failed to *read* the questions correctly.

7) Answer all questions

Unless you have been instructed that a penalty will be deducted for incorrect answers, it is better to guess than to omit a question.

8) Speed tests

It is often better NOT to guess on speed tests. It has been found that on timed tests people are tempted to spend the last few seconds before time is called in marking answers at random – without even reading them – in the hope of picking up a few extra points. To discourage this practice, the instructions may warn you that your score will be "corrected" for guessing. That is, a penalty will be applied. The incorrect answers will be deducted from the correct ones, or some other penalty formula will be used.

9) Review your answers

If you finish before time is called, go back to the questions you guessed or omitted to give them further thought. Review other answers if you have time.

10) Return your test materials

If you are ready to leave before others have finished or time is called, take ALL your materials to the monitor and leave quietly. Never take any test material with you. The monitor can discover whose papers are not complete, and taking a test booklet may be grounds for disqualification.

VIII. EXAMINATION TECHNIQUES

1) Read the general instructions carefully. These are usually printed on the first page of the exam booklet. As a rule, these instructions refer to the timing of the examination; the fact that you should not start work until the signal and must stop work at a signal, etc. If there are any *special* instructions, such as a choice of questions to be answered, make sure that you note this instruction carefully.

2) When you are ready to start work on the examination, that is as soon as the signal has been given, read the instructions to each question booklet, underline any key words or phrases, such as *least, best, outline, describe* and the like. In this way you will tend to answer as requested rather than discover on reviewing your paper that you *listed without describing*, that you selected the *worst* choice rather than the *best* choice, etc.

3) If the examination is of the objective or multiple-choice type – that is, each question will also give a series of possible answers: A, B, C or D, and you are called upon to select the best answer and write the letter next to that answer on your answer paper – it is advisable to start answering each question in turn. There may be anywhere from 50 to 100 such questions in the three or four hours allotted and you can see how much time would be taken if you read through all the questions before beginning to answer any. Furthermore, if you come across a question or group of questions which you know would be difficult to answer, it would undoubtedly affect your handling of all the other questions.

4) If the examination is of the essay type and contains but a few questions, it is a moot point as to whether you should read all the questions before starting to answer any one. Of course, if you are given a choice – say five out of seven and the like – then it is essential to read all the questions so you can eliminate the two that are most difficult. If, however, you are asked to answer all the questions, there may be danger in trying to answer the easiest one first because you may find that you will spend too much time on it. The best technique is to answer the first question, then proceed to the second, etc.

5) Time your answers. Before the exam begins, write down the time it started, then add the time allowed for the examination and write down the time it must be completed, then divide the time available somewhat as follows:
    - If 3-1/2 hours are allowed, that would be 210 minutes. If you have 80 objective-type questions, that would be an average of 2-1/2 minutes per question. Allow yourself no more than 2 minutes per question, or a total of 160 minutes, which will permit about 50 minutes to review.
    - If for the time allotment of 210 minutes there are 7 essay questions to answer, that would average about 30 minutes a question. Give yourself only 25 minutes per question so that you have about 35 minutes to review.

6) The most important instruction is to *read each question* and make sure you know what is wanted. The second most important instruction is to *time yourself properly* so that you answer every question. The third most important instruction is to *answer every question*. Guess if you have to but include something for each question. Remember that you will receive no credit for a blank and will probably receive some credit if you write something in answer to an essay question. If you guess a letter – say "B" for a multiple-choice question – you may have guessed right. If you leave a blank as an answer to a multiple-choice question, the examiners may respect your feelings but it will not add a point to your score. Some exams may penalize you for wrong answers, so in such cases *only*, you may not want to guess unless you have some basis for your answer.

7) Suggestions
    a. Objective-type questions
        1. Examine the question booklet for proper sequence of pages and questions
        2. Read all instructions carefully
        3. Skip any question which seems too difficult; return to it after all other questions have been answered
        4. Apportion your time properly; do not spend too much time on any single question or group of questions

5. Note and underline key words – *all, most, fewest, least, best, worst, same, opposite,* etc.
6. Pay particular attention to negatives
7. Note unusual option, e.g., unduly long, short, complex, different or similar in content to the body of the question
8. Observe the use of "hedging" words – *probably, may, most likely,* etc.
9. Make sure that your answer is put next to the same number as the question
10. Do not second-guess unless you have good reason to believe the second answer is definitely more correct
11. Cross out original answer if you decide another answer is more accurate; do not erase until you are ready to hand your paper in
12. Answer all questions; guess unless instructed otherwise
13. Leave time for review

b. Essay questions
1. Read each question carefully
2. Determine exactly what is wanted. Underline key words or phrases.
3. Decide on outline or paragraph answer
4. Include many different points and elements unless asked to develop any one or two points or elements
5. Show impartiality by giving pros and cons unless directed to select one side only
6. Make and write down any assumptions you find necessary to answer the questions
7. Watch your English, grammar, punctuation and choice of words
8. Time your answers; don't crowd material

8) Answering the essay question

Most essay questions can be answered by framing the specific response around several key words or ideas. Here are a few such key words or ideas:

M's: manpower, materials, methods, money, management
P's: purpose, program, policy, plan, procedure, practice, problems, pitfalls, personnel, public relations

a. Six basic steps in handling problems:
1. Preliminary plan and background development
2. Collect information, data and facts
3. Analyze and interpret information, data and facts
4. Analyze and develop solutions as well as make recommendations
5. Prepare report and sell recommendations
6. Install recommendations and follow up effectiveness

b. Pitfalls to avoid
1. *Taking things for granted* – A statement of the situation does not necessarily imply that each of the elements is necessarily true; for example, a complaint may be invalid and biased so that all that can be taken for granted is that a complaint has been registered

2. *Considering only one side of a situation* – Wherever possible, indicate several alternatives and then point out the reasons you selected the best one
3. *Failing to indicate follow up* – Whenever your answer indicates action on your part, make certain that you will take proper follow-up action to see how successful your recommendations, procedures or actions turn out to be
4. *Taking too long in answering any single question* – Remember to time your answers properly

IX. AFTER THE TEST

Scoring procedures differ in detail among civil service jurisdictions although the general principles are the same. Whether the papers are hand-scored or graded by machine we have described, they are nearly always graded by number. That is, the person who marks the paper knows only the number – never the name – of the applicant. Not until all the papers have been graded will they be matched with names. If other tests, such as training and experience or oral interview ratings have been given, scores will be combined. Different parts of the examination usually have different weights. For example, the written test might count 60 percent of the final grade, and a rating of training and experience 40 percent. In many jurisdictions, veterans will have a certain number of points added to their grades.

After the final grade has been determined, the names are placed in grade order and an eligible list is established. There are various methods for resolving ties between those who get the same final grade – probably the most common is to place first the name of the person whose application was received first. Job offers are made from the eligible list in the order the names appear on it. You will be notified of your grade and your rank as soon as all these computations have been made. This will be done as rapidly as possible.

People who are found to meet the requirements in the announcement are called "eligibles." Their names are put on a list of eligible candidates. An eligible's chances of getting a job depend on how high he stands on this list and how fast agencies are filling jobs from the list.

When a job is to be filled from a list of eligibles, the agency asks for the names of people on the list of eligibles for that job. When the civil service commission receives this request, it sends to the agency the names of the three people highest on this list. Or, if the job to be filled has specialized requirements, the office sends the agency the names of the top three persons who meet these requirements from the general list.

The appointing officer makes a choice from among the three people whose names were sent to him. If the selected person accepts the appointment, the names of the others are put back on the list to be considered for future openings.

That is the rule in hiring from all kinds of eligible lists, whether they are for typist, carpenter, chemist, or something else. For every vacancy, the appointing officer has his choice of any one of the top three eligibles on the list. This explains why the person whose name is on top of the list sometimes does not get an appointment when some of the persons lower on the list do. If the appointing officer chooses the second or third eligible, the No. 1 eligible does not get a job at once, but stays on the list until he is appointed or the list is terminated.

X. HOW TO PASS THE INTERVIEW TEST

The examination for which you applied requires an oral interview test. You have already taken the written test and you are now being called for the interview test – the final part of the formal examination.

You may think that it is not possible to prepare for an interview test and that there are no procedures to follow during an interview. Our purpose is to point out some things you can do in advance that will help you and some good rules to follow and pitfalls to avoid while you are being interviewed.

What is an interview supposed to test?

The written examination is designed to test the technical knowledge and competence of the candidate; the oral is designed to evaluate intangible qualities, not readily measured otherwise, and to establish a list showing the relative fitness of each candidate – as measured against his competitors – for the position sought. Scoring is not on the basis of "right" and "wrong," but on a sliding scale of values ranging from "not passable" to "outstanding." As a matter of fact, it is possible to achieve a relatively low score without a single "incorrect" answer because of evident weakness in the qualities being measured.

Occasionally, an examination may consist entirely of an oral test – either an individual or a group oral. In such cases, information is sought concerning the technical knowledges and abilities of the candidate, since there has been no written examination for this purpose. More commonly, however, an oral test is used to supplement a written examination.

Who conducts interviews?

The composition of oral boards varies among different jurisdictions. In nearly all, a representative of the personnel department serves as chairman. One of the members of the board may be a representative of the department in which the candidate would work. In some cases, "outside experts" are used, and, frequently, a businessman or some other representative of the general public is asked to serve. Labor and management or other special groups may be represented. The aim is to secure the services of experts in the appropriate field.

However the board is composed, it is a good idea (and not at all improper or unethical) to ascertain in advance of the interview who the members are and what groups they represent. When you are introduced to them, you will have some idea of their backgrounds and interests, and at least you will not stutter and stammer over their names.

What should be done before the interview?

While knowledge about the board members is useful and takes some of the surprise element out of the interview, there is other preparation which is more substantive. It *is* possible to prepare for an oral interview – in several ways:

1) Keep a copy of your application and review it carefully before the interview

This may be the only document before the oral board, and the starting point of the interview. Know what education and experience you have listed there, and the sequence and dates of all of it. Sometimes the board will ask you to review the highlights of your experience for them; you should not have to hem and haw doing it.

2) Study the class specification and the examination announcement

Usually, the oral board has one or both of these to guide them. The qualities, characteristics or knowledges required by the position sought are stated in these documents. They offer valuable clues as to the nature of the oral interview. For example, if the job involves supervisory responsibilities, the announcement will usually indicate that knowledge of modern supervisory methods and the qualifications of the candidate as a supervisor will be tested. If so, you can expect such questions, frequently in the form of a hypothetical situation which you are expected to solve. NEVER go into an oral without knowledge of the duties and responsibilities of the job you seek.

3) Think through each qualification required

Try to visualize the kind of questions you would ask if you were a board member. How well could you answer them? Try especially to appraise your own knowledge and background in each area, *measured against the job sought*, and identify any areas in which you are weak. Be critical and realistic – do not flatter yourself.

4) Do some general reading in areas in which you feel you may be weak

For example, if the job involves supervision and your past experience has NOT, some general reading in supervisory methods and practices, particularly in the field of human relations, might be useful. Do NOT study agency procedures or detailed manuals. The oral board will be testing your understanding and capacity, not your memory.

5) Get a good night's sleep and watch your general health and mental attitude

You will want a clear head at the interview. Take care of a cold or any other minor ailment, and of course, no hangovers.

What should be done on the day of the interview?

Now comes the day of the interview itself. Give yourself plenty of time to get there. Plan to arrive somewhat ahead of the scheduled time, particularly if your appointment is in the fore part of the day. If a previous candidate fails to appear, the board might be ready for you a bit early. By early afternoon an oral board is almost invariably behind schedule if there are many candidates, and you may have to wait. Take along a book or magazine to read, or your application to review, but leave any extraneous material in the waiting room when you go in for your interview. In any event, relax and compose yourself.

The matter of dress is important. The board is forming impressions about you – from your experience, your manners, your attitude, and your appearance. Give your personal appearance careful attention. Dress your best, but not your flashiest. Choose conservative, appropriate clothing, and be sure it is immaculate. This is a business interview, and your appearance should indicate that you regard it as such. Besides, being well groomed and properly dressed will help boost your confidence.

Sooner or later, someone will call your name and escort you into the interview room. *This is it.* From here on you are on your own. It is too late for any more preparation. But remember, you asked for this opportunity to prove your fitness, and you are here because your request was granted.

What happens when you go in?

The usual sequence of events will be as follows: The clerk (who is often the board stenographer) will introduce you to the chairman of the oral board, who will introduce you to the other members of the board. Acknowledge the introductions before you sit down. Do not be surprised if you find a microphone facing you or a stenotypist sitting by. Oral interviews are usually recorded in the event of an appeal or other review.

Usually the chairman of the board will open the interview by reviewing the highlights of your education and work experience from your application – primarily for the benefit of the other members of the board, as well as to get the material into the record. Do not interrupt or comment unless there is an error or significant misinterpretation; if that is the case, do not hesitate. But do not quibble about insignificant matters. Also, he will usually ask you some question about your education, experience or your present job – partly to get you to start talking and to establish the interviewing "rapport." He may start the actual questioning, or turn it over to one of the other members. Frequently, each member undertakes the questioning on a particular area, one in which he is perhaps most competent, so you can expect each member to participate in the examination. Because time is limited, you may also expect some rather abrupt switches in the direction the questioning takes, so do not be upset by it. Normally, a board member will not pursue a single line of questioning unless he discovers a particular strength or weakness.

After each member has participated, the chairman will usually ask whether any member has any further questions, then will ask you if you have anything you wish to add. Unless you are expecting this question, it may floor you. Worse, it may start you off on an extended, extemporaneous speech. The board is not usually seeking more information. The question is principally to offer you a last opportunity to present further qualifications or to indicate that you have nothing to add. So, if you feel that a significant qualification or characteristic has been overlooked, it is proper to point it out in a sentence or so. Do not compliment the board on the thoroughness of their examination – they have been sketchy, and you know it. If you wish, merely say, "No thank you, I have nothing further to add." This is a point where you can "talk yourself out" of a good impression or fail to present an important bit of information. Remember, *you close the interview yourself*.

The chairman will then say, "That is all, Mr. _____, thank you." Do not be startled; the interview is over, and quicker than you think. Thank him, gather your belongings and take your leave. Save your sigh of relief for the other side of the door.

How to put your best foot forward

Throughout this entire process, you may feel that the board individually and collectively is trying to pierce your defenses, seek out your hidden weaknesses and embarrass and confuse you. Actually, this is not true. They are obliged to make an appraisal of your qualifications for the job you are seeking, and they want to see you in your best light. Remember, they must interview all candidates and a non-cooperative candidate may become a failure in spite of their best efforts to bring out his qualifications. Here are 15 suggestions that will help you:

1) Be natural – Keep your attitude confident, not cocky

If you are not confident that you can do the job, do not expect the board to be. Do not apologize for your weaknesses, try to bring out your strong points. The board is interested in a positive, not negative, presentation. Cockiness will antagonize any board member and make him wonder if you are covering up a weakness by a false show of strength.

2) Get comfortable, but don't lounge or sprawl

Sit erectly but not stiffly. A careless posture may lead the board to conclude that you are careless in other things, or at least that you are not impressed by the importance of the occasion. Either conclusion is natural, even if incorrect. Do not fuss with your clothing, a pencil or an ashtray. Your hands may occasionally be useful to emphasize a point; do not let them become a point of distraction.

3) Do not wisecrack or make small talk

This is a serious situation, and your attitude should show that you consider it as such. Further, the time of the board is limited – they do not want to waste it, and neither should you.

4) Do not exaggerate your experience or abilities

In the first place, from information in the application or other interviews and sources, the board may know more about you than you think. Secondly, you probably will not get away with it. An experienced board is rather adept at spotting such a situation, so do not take the chance.

5) If you know a board member, do not make a point of it, yet do not hide it

Certainly you are not fooling him, and probably not the other members of the board. Do not try to take advantage of your acquaintanceship – it will probably do you little good.

6) Do not dominate the interview

Let the board do that. They will give you the clues – do not assume that you have to do all the talking. Realize that the board has a number of questions to ask you, and do not try to take up all the interview time by showing off your extensive knowledge of the answer to the first one.

7) Be attentive

You only have 20 minutes or so, and you should keep your attention at its sharpest throughout. When a member is addressing a problem or question to you, give him your undivided attention. Address your reply principally to him, but do not exclude the other board members.

8) Do not interrupt

A board member may be stating a problem for you to analyze. He will ask you a question when the time comes. Let him state the problem, and wait for the question.

9) Make sure you understand the question

Do not try to answer until you are sure what the question is. If it is not clear, restate it in your own words or ask the board member to clarify it for you. However, do not haggle about minor elements.

10) Reply promptly but not hastily

A common entry on oral board rating sheets is "candidate responded readily," or "candidate hesitated in replies." Respond as promptly and quickly as you can, but do not jump to a hasty, ill-considered answer.

11) Do not be peremptory in your answers

A brief answer is proper – but do not fire your answer back. That is a losing game from your point of view. The board member can probably ask questions much faster than you can answer them.

12) Do not try to create the answer you think the board member wants

He is interested in what kind of mind you have and how it works – not in playing games. Furthermore, he can usually spot this practice and will actually grade you down on it.

13) Do not switch sides in your reply merely to agree with a board member

Frequently, a member will take a contrary position merely to draw you out and to see if you are willing and able to defend your point of view. Do not start a debate, yet do not surrender a good position. If a position is worth taking, it is worth defending.

14) Do not be afraid to admit an error in judgment if you are shown to be wrong

The board knows that you are forced to reply without any opportunity for careful consideration. Your answer may be demonstrably wrong. If so, admit it and get on with the interview.

15) Do not dwell at length on your present job

The opening question may relate to your present assignment. Answer the question but do not go into an extended discussion. You are being examined for a *new* job, not your present one. As a matter of fact, try to phrase ALL your answers in terms of the job for which you are being examined.

Basis of Rating

Probably you will forget most of these "do's" and "don'ts" when you walk into the oral interview room. Even remembering them all will not ensure you a passing grade. Perhaps you did not have the qualifications in the first place. But remembering them will help you to put your best foot forward, without treading on the toes of the board members.

Rumor and popular opinion to the contrary notwithstanding, an oral board wants you to make the best appearance possible. They know you are under pressure – but they also want to see how you respond to it as a guide to what your reaction would be under the pressures of the job you seek. They will be influenced by the degree of poise you display, the personal traits you show and the manner in which you respond.

ABOUT THIS BOOK

This book contains tests divided into Examination Sections. Go through each test, answering every question in the margin. We have also attached a sample answer sheet at the back of the book that can be removed and used. At the end of each test look at the answer key and check your answers. On the ones you got wrong, look at the right answer choice and learn. Do not fill in the answers first. Do not memorize the questions and answers, but understand the answer and principles involved. On your test, the questions will likely be different from the samples. Questions are changed and new ones added. If you understand these past questions you should have success with any changes that arise. Tests may consist of several types of questions. We have additional books on each subject should more study be advisable or necessary for you. Finally, the more you study, the better prepared you will be. This book is intended to be the last thing you study before you walk into the examination room. Prior study of relevant texts is also recommended. NLC publishes some of these in our Fundamental Series. Knowledge and good sense are important factors in passing your exam. Good luck also helps. So now study this Passbook, absorb the material contained within and take that knowledge into the examination. Then do your best to pass that exam.

EXAMINATION SECTION

EXAMINATION SECTION
TEST 1

DIRECTIONS: Each question or incomplete statement is followed by several suggested answers or completions. Select the one that BEST answers the question or completes the statement. *PRINT THE LETTER OF THE CORRECT ANSWER IN THE SPACE AT THE RIGHT.*

1. The administrator who allows his staff to suggest ways to do their work will usually find that

    A. this practice contributes to high productivity
    B. the administrator's ideas produce greater output
    C. clerical employees suggest inefficient work methods
    D. subordinate employees resent performing a management function

    1._____

2. In considering how to distribute among employees the various tasks which must be accomplished, an administrator should bear in mind that MOST people

    A. are working mainly for money, so the particular task they do is usually unimportant
    B. would rather work with a congenial group, but since this lowers output, it is better to have people work alone
    C. want recognition as outstanding workers, but since only one can be best, it is better policy to stress equality
    D. are concerned with being part of a group and also hope to be outstanding, and the administrator must consider both

    2._____

3. A coordinator may be the supervisor of several employees. As such, he is their leader. The style of leadership which is MOST effective is a style in which

    A. the coordinator's behavior is tailored to the situation
    B. the coordinator lets his subordinates solve their own problems
    C. the coordinator consults with his subordinates about any work being done
    D. subordinates are told firmly what to do, how and when

    3._____

4. As a coordinator you may be required to set up a records retention program. To set up such a program, the FIRST step you should take is to

    A. find out how long the records will be needed
    B. determine what types of records are maintained
    C. investigate storage facilities
    D. revise the filing system

    4._____

5. You are responsible for supervising the work of several subordinates who deal directly with people seeking specific help from your department. One of your subordinates is faced with an angry citizen who has brought his troubles to the wrong department, but who refuses to believe this and is loudly demanding to *see the manager*. The subordinate asks you to step in and take over. Which of the following is probably the MOST effective way of handling this situation?

    A. Tell your subordinate that since this is obviously not a matter for your department, his request that you take over is inappropriate.
    B. Remind your subordinate firmly that it is his job to deal with the public, and that he must learn to handle people who are confused and angry.
    C. Do not stop what you are doing, but call out to the angry citizen that whatever your subordinate told him is correct.
    D. Step in and direct the angry citizen to a department which can help him.

6. A supervisor is one who is responsible for the actions of others working for him and at the same time is responsible to others above him in the organization chart.
The foregoing statement IMPLIES, in effect, that the supervisor

    A. has full authority for his actions
    B. can delegate his responsibilities to his assistants
    C. accepts direction from his own supervisor
    D. has higher status than a coordinator

7. In issuing requested supplies to employees of the office, there is a great deal of merit in limiting the quantity issued at any one time to about a two-week supply.
In MOST cases, this policy is

    A. *bad,* because employees should be allowed as large a quantity of supplies as they feel they need
    B. *bad,* because, if larger quantities were issued, employees would have to ask for supplies less often
    C. *good,* because the smaller the quantity issued, the more efficiently the office can be managed
    D. *good,* because a larger amount would encourage waste and a smaller amount would necessitate more trips to the stockroom

8. As a coordinator, assume that there is a rule in your office that all correspondence to other agencies must be signed personally by the hearing officer.
If the hearing officer is unexpectedly absent on a day when an important letter which has not yet been signed is scheduled to be mailed out, the MOST appropriate action for you to take is to

    A. seek advice from the superior of the hearing officer
    B. sign the letter with the name of the hearing officer and your own initials
    C. telephone the hearing officer at home
    D. wait until the next day

9. Unless otherwise directed, a car should be parked parallel to and within 12 inches of a curb or edge of a roadway, facing in the same direction as traffic on the car's side of the road.
   Of the following, the MOST likely reason for this regulation is to

   A. allow the car's passengers adequate room to open its doors
   B. make sure that the road can be washed effectively by Sanitation Department equipment
   C. prevent the car from blocking the smooth flow of traffic
   D. allow another vehicle enough room to double-park

9.____

10. Parking meters are generally installed in shopping and commercial districts.
    Of the following, the MOST likely reason for this practice is to

    A. promote an equitable rotation of short-term parking opportunities
    B. prevent trucks from stopping to unload and receive deliveries
    C. discourage overnight parking of vehicles by local residents
    D. maximize the revenue gained from these meters to offset the cost of purchasing and maintaining them

10.____

11. In the city, the large numbers of criminal cases have made it difficult for the court system to assure a defendant a speedy trial.
    The MAIN result of this situation has been that

    A. judges are imposing longer sentences to reduce the number of cases
    B. defense attorneys and prosecutors often engage in plea bargaining
    C. judges are being selected more rapidly by special *blue-ribbon* panels
    D. juries are now given a limit of 48 hours within which they must deliver a verdict

11.____

12. The transit fare in the city may have to be raised to meet higher transit authority costs.
    The one of the following which is MOST likely to be the PRINCIPAL cause of such higher costs is

    A. equipment repair
    B. equipment replacement
    C. salary increases
    D. conversion to air conditioning

12.____

Questions 13–16.

DIRECTIONS: Questions 13 through 16 are to be answered on the basis of the following table.

AVERAGE HOURLY CARRYING CAPACITIES OF
SINGLE-LANE TRANSPORT FACILITIES

MODE OF TRANSPORT	NO. OF PASSENGERS
Autos on surface streets	1,575
Autos on elevated highways	2,025
Buses on surface streets	9,000
Streetcars on surface streets	13,500
Streetcars in subways	20,000
Local subway trains	40,000
Express subway trains	60,000

13. For a group of elevated highways to approximately equal the carrying capacity of a two-lane local subway train facility, the TOTAL number of lanes required would be MOST NEARLY

    A. 80 B. 60 C. 40 D. 20

14. Buses on surface streets using a single lane can carry approximately what percentage of the passengers that express subway trains in one lane can carry?

    A. 20% B. 15% C. 10% D. 5%

15. The average number of passengers that can be carried by autos on surface streets in one day is MOST NEARLY

    A. 1,575 B. 2,025 C. 37,800 D. 48,600

16. If one lane of a surface street were used for buses and another lane were used for streetcars, the number of passengers that could be carried by both lanes together in one hour would probably be MOST NEARLY

    A. 9,000 B. 11,250 C. 13,500 D. 22,500

17. The one of the following which is MOST likely to result from a change from a centralized plan for records management to a decentralized plan is

    A. a loss of time for personnel who use the records
    B. greater specialization of record keeping personnel
    C. authority and responsibility for the records management program being vested in one person within the organization
    D. easier access to the records for personnel most concerned with such records

18. The *grapevine* is an informal means of communication in an organization.
    The attitude of a supervisor with respect to the grapevine should be to

    A. ignore it since it deals mainly with rumors and sensational information
    B. regard it as a serious danger which should be eliminated
    C. accept it as a real line of communications which should be listened to
    D. utilize it for most purposes instead of the official line of communication

19. The supervisor of an office that must deal with the public should realize that planning in this type of work situation

    A. is useless because he does not know how many people will request service or what service they will request
    B. must be done at a higher level but that he should be ready to implement the results of such planning
    C. is useful primarily for those activities that are not concerned with public contact
    D. is useful for all the activities of the office, including those that relate to public contact

20. Which of the following factors is MOST important in planning the location of work stations and other aspects of office layout? 20._____
    A. Preferences of the office employees
    B. Nature and flow of work in the office
    C. Volume of work in the office
    D. Seniority of employees in the office

KEY (CORRECT ANSWERS)

1.	A	11.	B
2.	D	12.	C
3.	A	13.	C
4.	B	14.	B
5.	D	15.	C
6.	C	16.	D
7.	D	17.	D
8.	A	18.	C
9.	C	19.	D
10.	A	20.	B

TEST 2

DIRECTIONS: Each question or incomplete statement is followed by several suggested answers or completions. Select the one that BEST answers the question or completes the statement. *PRINT THE LETTER OF THE CORRECT ANSWER IN THE SPACE AT THE RIGHT.*

1. It is usually MOST desirable for a work supervisor for a large group of clerical workers to have a work station which

    A. provides a view of the entire room
    B. is in another room away from all the clerical workers
    C. is isolated from all workers except for a secretary or assistant
    D. is located so that he can receive all visitors

1._____

Questions 2-5.

DIRECTIONS: Questions 2 through 5 must be answered on the basis of the following passage.

Analysis of current data reveals that motor vehicle transportation actually requires less space than was used for other types of transportation in the pre-automobile era, even including the substantial area taken by freeways. The reason is that when the fast moving through traffic is put on built-for-the-purpose arterial roads, then the amount of ordinary space needed for strictly local movement and for access to property drops sharply. Even the amount of land taken for urban expressways turns out to be surprisingly small in terms either of total urban acreage or of the volume of traffic they carry. No existing or contemplated urban expressway system requires as much as 3 percent of the land in the areas it serves, and this would be exceptionally high. The Los Angeles freeway system occupies only 2 percent of the available land; the same is true of the District of Columbia, where only 0.75 percent is pavement, with the remaining 1.25 percent as open space. California studies estimate that, in a typical California urban community, 1.6 to 2 percent of the area should be devoted to freeways, which will handle 50 to 60 percent of all traffic needs, and about ten times as much land to the ordinary roads and streets that carry the rest of the traffic. By comparison, when John A. Sutter laid out Sacramento in 1850, he provided 38 percent of the area for streets and sidewalks. The French architect, Pierre L' Enfant, proposed 59 percent of the area of the District of Columbia for roads and streets; urban renewal in Southwest Washington, incorporating a modern street network, reduced the acreage of space for pedestrian and vehicular traffic in the renewal area from 48.2 to 41.5 percent of the total. If we are to have a reasoned consideration of the impact of highway transportation on contemporary urban development, it would be well to understand these relationships.

2. The passage states that

    A. modern transportation uses less space than was used for transportation before the auto age
    B. expressways require more space than streets in terms of urban acreage
    C. typical urban communities were poorly designed in terms of relationship between space used for traffic and that used for other purposes
    D. the need for local and access roads would increase if the number of expressways were increased

2._____

3. According to the above passage, it was originally planned that the percent of the area to be used for roads and streets in the District of Columbia should be MOST NEARLY

    A. 40%   B. 45%   C. 50%   D. 60%

3._____

4. The above passage states that the amount of space needed for local traffic

   A. *increases* when arterial highways are constructed
   B. *decreases* when arterial highways are constructed
   C. *decreases* when there is more land available
   D. *increases* when there is more land available

5. According to the above passage, studies estimate that, in a typical California urban community, the amount of land devoted to ordinary roads and streets as compared with that devoted to freeways should be MOST NEARLY _____ as much.

   A. one-half   B. one-tenth
   C. twice   D. ten times

Questions 6–8.

DIRECTIONS: Questions 6 through 8 must be answered on the basis of the following passage.

A glaring exception to the usual practice of the judicial trial as a means of conflict resolution is the utilization of administrative hearings. The growing tendency to create administrative bodies with rule-making and quasi-judicial powers has shattered many standard concepts. A comprehensive examination of the legal process cannot neglect these newer patterns.

In the administrative process, the legislative, executive, and judicial functions are mixed together, and many functions, such as investigating, advocating, negotiating, testifying, rule-making, and adjudicating, are carried out by the same agency. The reason for the breakdown of the separation-of-powers formula is not hard to find. It was felt by Congress, and state and municipal legislatures, that certain regulatory tasks could not be performed efficiently, rapidly, expertly, and with due concern for the public interest by the traditional branches of government. Accordingly, regulatory agencies were delegated powers to consider disputes from the earliest stage of investigation to the final stages of adjudication entirely within each agency itself, subject only to limited review in the regular courts.

6. The above passage states that the usual means for conflict resolution is through the use of

   A. judicial trial   B. administrative hearing
   C. legislation   D. regulatory agencies

7. The above passage *implies* that the use of administrative hearing in resolving conflict is a(n) _____ approach.

   A. traditional   B. new
   C. dangerous   D. experimental

8. The above passage states that the reason for the breakdown of the separation-of-powers formula in the administrative process is that

   A. Congress believed that certain regulatory tasks could be better performed by separate agencies
   B. legislative and executive functions are incompatible in the same agency
   C. investigative and regulatory functions are not normally reviewed by the courts
   D. state and municipal legislatures are more concerned with efficiency than with legality

9. An employee examining the summonses of individuals appearing for hearings noticed that the address on one summons was the same as that of an individual who had appeared earlier that day. He asked the second respondent if he knew the first respondent.
The MOST appropriate evaluation of the employee's behavior is that he should

   A. not have mentioned any other respondent to the second respondent
   B. not waste time inspecting summonses in such detail
   C. be commended for inspecting summonses so carefully
   D. be commended for his investigation of the respondents

10. An employee is assigned to maintain all types of frequently used reference material such as booklets and technical papers. He keeps these in a pile on a shelf in order of arrival. When new material arrives, he puts it on top of the pile.
Which of the following BEST evaluates the employee's handling of this reference material?
His system is most likely to result in _____ filing and _____ retrieval.

   A. fast; slow
   B. slow; slow
   C. fast; fast
   D. slow; fast

11. An employee computes statistics relating to proceedings. The method he devised consists of organizing his source and summary documents in such a manner that at any time another employee can assume the work. This method takes a little more time than other possible methods.
Which of the following statements BEST evaluates the judgment of the employee in devising such a method?
The employee has used

   A. *good* judgment because it is important to provide for continuity
   B. *poor* judgment because he is not using the fastest method
   C. *good* judgment because if a job is done as fast as possible, it becomes tiring
   D. *poor* judgment because it is not an employee's responsibility to prepare for a replacement

12. Assume that it is your job to receive incoming telephone calls. Those calls which you cannot handle yourself have to be transferred to the appropriate office.
If you receive an outside call for an extension line which is busy, the one of the following which you should do FIRST is to

   A. interrupt the person speaking on the extension and tell him a call is waiting
   B. tell the caller the line is busy and let him know every thirty seconds whether or not it is free
   C. leave the caller on *hold* until the extension is free
   D. tell the caller the line is busy and ask him if he wishes to wait

13. On one occasion in a certain office, an elderly employee collapsed, apparently the victim of a heart attack. Chaos broke out in the office as several people tried to help him, and several others tried to get assistance.
    Of the following, the MOST certain way of avoiding such chaos in the future is to

    A. keep a copy of heart attack procedures on file so that it can be referred to by any member of the staff when an emergency occurs
    B. provide each member of the staff with a first aid book which is to be kept in an accessible location
    C. train all members of the staff in the proper procedure for handling such emergencies, assigning specific responsibilities
    D. post, in several places around the office, a list of specific procedures to follow in each of several different emergencies

13.____

14. Your superior has subscribed to several publications directly related to your division's work, and he has asked you to see to it that the publications are circulated among the supervisory personnel in the division. There are eight supervisors involved.
    The BEST method of insuring that all eight see these publications is to

    A. place the publication in the division's general reference library as soon as it arrives
    B. inform each supervisor whenever a publication arrives and remind all of them that they are responsible for reading it
    C. prepare a standard slip that can be stapled to each publication, listing the eight supervisors and saying, *Please read, initial your name, and pass along*
    D. send a memo to the eight supervisors saying that they may wish to purchase individual subscriptions in their own names if they are interested in seeing each issue

14.____

15. Assume that you have been asked to prepare a narrative summary of the monthly reports submitted by employees in your division.
    In preparing your summary of this month's reports, the FIRST step to take is to

    A. read through the reports, noting their general content and any unusual features
    B. decide how many typewritten pages your summary should contain
    C. make a written summary of each separate report, so that you will not have to go back to the original reports again
    D. ask each employee which points he would prefer to see emphasized in your summary

15.____

16. Your superior has telephoned a number of key officials in your agency to ask whether they can meet at a certain time next month. He has found that they can all make it, and he has asked you to confirm the meeting.
    Which of the following is the BEST way to confirm such a meeting?

    A. Note the meeting on your superior's calendar
    B. Post a notice of the meeting on the agency bulletin board
    C. Call the officials on the day of the meeting to remind them of the meeting
    D. Write a memo to each official involved repeating the time and place of the meeting

16.____

17. Of the following, the worker who is MOST likely to create a problem in maintaining safety is one who

    A. disregards hazards
    B. feels tired
    C. resents authority
    D. gets bored

17.____

18. Assume that a new regulation requires that certain kinds of private organizations file information forms with your department. You have been asked to write the short explanatory message that will be printed on the front cover of the pamphlet containing the forms and instructions.
Which of the following would be the MOST appropriate way of beginning this message?

    A. Get the readers' attention by emphasizing immediately that there are legal penalties for organizations that fail to file before a certain date
    B. Briefly state the nature of the enclosed forms and the types of organizations that must file
    C. Say that your department is very sorry to have to put organizations to such an inconvenience
    D. Quote the entire regulation adopted by the city, even if it is quite long and is expressed in complicated legal language

18.____

19. Suppose that you have been told to make up the vacation schedule for the 15 employees in a particular unit. In order for the unit to operate effectively, only a few employees can be on vacation at the same time.
Which of the following is the MOST advisable approach in making up the schedule?

    A. Draw up a schedule assigning vacations in alphabetical order
    B. Find out when the supervisors want to take their vacations, and randomly assign whatever periods are left to the non-supervisory personnel
    C. Assign the most desirable times to employees of longest standing, and the least desirable times to the newest employees
    D. Have all employees state their own preference, and then work out any conflicts in consultation with the people involved

19.____

20. Assume that you have been asked to prepare job descriptions for various positions in your department.
Which of the following are the BASIC points that should be covered in a job description?

    A. General duties and responsibilities of the position, with examples of day-to-day tasks
    B. Comments on the performances of present employees
    C. Estimates of the number of openings that may be available in each category during the coming year
    D. Instructions for carrying out the specific tasks assigned to your department

20.____

KEY (CORRECT ANSWERS)

1. A
2. A
3. D
4. B
5. D

6. A
7. B
8. A
9. A
10. A

11. A
12. D
13. C
14. C
15. A

16. D
17. A
18. B
19. D
20. A

EXAMINATION SECTION
TEST 1

DIRECTIONS: Each question or incomplete statement is followed by several suggested answers or completions. Select the one that BEST answers the question or completes the Statement. *PRINT THE LETTER OF THE CORRECT ANSWER IN THE SPACE AT THE RIGHT.*

1. Your superior has asked you to notify division employees of an important change in one of the operating procedures described in the division manual. Every employee presently has a copy of this manual.
Which of the following is *normally* the MOST practical way to get the employees to understand such a change?

    A. Notify each employee individually of the change and answer any questions he might have
    B. Send a written notice to key personnel, directing them to inform the people under them
    C. Call a general meeting, distribute a corrected page for the manual, and discuss the change
    D. Send a memo to employees describing the change in general terms and asking them to make the necessary corrections in their copies of the manual

1.____

2. A supervisor was directed by the head of his division to report figures for overtime wages. The supervisor asked a clerk under his supervision to give him the figures, and he passed the clerk's figures along to his superior without questioning them. It was then discovered that the clerk had carelessly supplied the wrong information. Who can PROPERLY be held responsible for the mistake, the supervisor or the payroll clerk?

    A. Only the supervisor, because he should have known that the clerk would be careless
    B. Only the clerk, because it should be unnecessary for supervisors to check the work of their subordinates except for work which is unusually complex or important
    C. Neither of them, because it is perfectly understandable that such mistakes will occur from time to time
    D. Both of them, because the person to whom a task is delegated is responsible to the supervisor who delegated the task, and the supervisor is responsible to his superior

2.____

3. As a supervisor, it is necessary for you to show a new employee how to enter information on standard forms that he will have to prepare. These forms have a number of blanks to be filled in, but the job is fairly simple once a person becomes familiar with it.
The BEST way to show the new employee how to do the job is to

    A. explain how to do it and have him fill out a few forms, helping him with any difficulties
    B. give him a completed form to use as a model, and tell him to do all the others exactly the same way
    C. put him on his own immediately, and assume that he will learn for himself through trial and error
    D. give him several dozen completed forms to read, and ask him to check back with you in a few hours when he feels ready to start work

3.____

4. An administrative position carries with it a certain amount of authority. Management theorists feel that the exercise of authority is ESSENTIAL in carrying out the goals of an organization because

   A. administrators enjoy having the power to order people around, and they would not be willing to give it up
   B. administrators must work through others to accomplish objectives, so they must have the right to direct others to act in certain ways
   C. most employees are not able to carry out tasks on their own initiative, and they need a stern supervisor to make sure that the work gets done
   D. once authority is recognized, it can be carefully limited so that no administrator makes unreasonable demands or sets himself up as a petty tyrant

4.____

5. Assume that the work in your department involves the use of many technical terms. In such a situation, when you are answering inquiries from the general public, it would *usually* be BEST to

   A. use simple language and avoid the technical terms
   B. use the technical terms whenever possible
   C. use technical terms freely, but explain each term in parentheses
   D. apologize if you are forced to use a technical term

5.____

6. You are answering a letter that was written on the letterhead of the ABC Company and signed by James H. Block, Treasurer. What is usually considered to be the CORRECT salutation to use in your reply?
Dear

   A. ABC Company: B. Sirs:
   C. Mr. Block: D. Mr. Treasurer:

6.____

7. Assume that one of your duties is to handle routine letters of inquiry from the public. The one of the following which is *usually* considered to be MOST desirable in replying to such a letter is a

   A. detailed answer handwritten on the original letter of inquiry
   B. phone call, since you can cover details more easily over the phone than in a letter
   C. short letter giving the specific information requested
   D. long letter discussing all possible aspects of the questions raised

7.____

8. The CHIEF reason for dividing a letter into paragraphs is to

   A. make the message clear to the reader by starting a new paragraph for each new topic
   B. make a short letter occupy as much of the page as possible
   C. keep the reader's attention by providing a pause from time to time
   D. make the letter look neat and business like

8.____

9. Your superior has asked you to send a letter via fax from your agency to a government agency in another city. He has written the letter and provided you with all contact information.
Which of the following does not need to be included on the fax cover sheet to be sent along with your superior's letter?

    A. Today's date
    B. A final sentence such as, *We would appreciate hearing from your agency in reply as soon as is convenient for you*
    C. Name of the contact person or department at the other agency
    D. Name of sender

10. Suppose that a usually competent employee whom you supervise has suddenly begun having difficulty completing his assignments. You ask the employee to speak to you privately about this situation and he agrees that he would appreciate this opportunity because of a problem he is having.
Of the following, which one would be the BEST technique for you to use in speaking with him?

    A. Criticize the employee's performance as soon as he mentions his difficulty in completing his assignments
    B. Listen patiently to what the employee has to say before making any comments on your own
    C. Refuse to discuss any personal factors which the employee mentions when he tries to explain his recent work difficulty
    D. Allow the employee to argue with you but plan your attack and defense carefully

11. Suppose that you receive a telephone call from someone identifying himself as an employee in another department who asks to be given information which your own department regards as confidential.
Which of the following is the BEST way of handling such a request?

    A. Give the information requested, since your caller has official standing
    B. Grant the request, provided the caller gives you a signed receipt
    C. Refuse the request, because you have no way of knowing whether the caller is really who he claims to be
    D. Explain that the information is confidential and inform the caller of the channels he must go through to have the information released to him

12. The MAIN purpose of transferring materials from active to inactive files is to

    A. keep current reference files from growing to a size where they become inefficient and unmanageable
    B. distinguish between important business and less important matters
    C. provide a means of storing letters that need not be answered
    D. make sure that there is some way of retrieving information from previous years

13. The one of the following for which a cross-index is MOST likely to be needed is a

    A. file of reference material arranged by subject
    B. file of individual personnel records arranged alphabetically
    C. card file containing addresses and phone numbers for various organizations
    D. supervisor's tickler file

14. The CHIEF advantage of a rotary file is that   14.____

    A. it holds much more material than a standard file cabinet
    B. it provides a temporary location for material that is due to be placed in the permanent files
    C. items can be easily located and scanned without being removed from the file
    D. less time is required for placing an item on a rotary file than for placing it in a standard upright file

15. Centralization of office activities has become an important technique for achieving   15.____
    greater efficiency in clerical work.
    Which of the following is NOT a result that could *normally* be gained by centralization of a clerical activity?

    A. More even distribution of work loads among employees performing the same kind of clerical tasks
    B. Increased opportunities for clerical workers to learn new skills and become better qualified for promotion to administrative positions
    C. Cost savings on office equipment whose use can now be shared by several employees
    D. Establishment of uniform standards and procedures for various clerical activities

16. Assume that certain work processed in your office is then sent to another office for further processing. One of the employees in your office tells you that the supervisor in the other office has been complaining about your office's method of handling the work.   16.____
    Of the following, the MOST appropriate action for you to take is to

    A. get all the details from the employee and then speak to the other supervisor
    B. ignore the situation and continue to do the best you can
    C. remind the supervisor that it is not his function to evaluate your work
    D. refrain from reporting the matter to your superior

17. It is the practice in your department to make objective evaluations of the performance of different units. This requires looking at the results achieved by a particular unit during a specified period of time—for instance, the number of applications processed, the number of inquiries answered, the number of inspections made, and so forth.   17.____
    Of the following, the BEST method of evaluating the performance of each unit is to compare its results with the

    A. results achieved by all units of the same size that are performing other kinds of work
    B. goals that the unit was reasonably expected to meet during the specified period
    C. performance of the same unit during a similar period of time four or five years earlier
    D. amount of money spent to achieve these results

18. It is possible that you may be asked to submit a brief written evaluation of the work of several employees under your supervision. Such an evaluation should *normally* give LEAST emphasis to an employee's   18.____

    A. attendance record, including tardiness and absence
    B. ability to grasp new assignments and carry them out effectively
    C. educational background and previous employment experience
    D. ability to get along with co-workers

19. You have been asked to help draw up a plan for a new operation to be carried out by your department. The INITIAL step in planning should be

    A. finding out how much money is available in the budget for the operation
    B. determining the objective or objectives of the operation
    C. gathering information on similar operations elsewhere
    D. determining the most reasonable way of structuring the operation

20. Studies show that office employees place high importance on the social and human aspects of the organization. What office employees like best about their jobs is the kind of people with whom they work. So strive hard to group people who are most likely to get along well together.
    Based on this statement, it is MOST reasonable to assume that office workers are most pleased to work in a group which

    A. is congenial
    B. has high productivity
    C. allows individual creativity
    D. is unlike other groups

KEY (CORRECT ANSWERS)

1.	C	11.	D
2.	D	12.	A
3.	A	13.	A
4.	B	14.	C
5.	A	15.	B
6.	C	16.	A
7.	C	17.	B
8.	A	18.	C
9.	B	19.	B
10.	B	20.	A

TEST 2

DIRECTIONS: Each question or incomplete statement is followed by several suggested answers or completions. Select the one that BEST answers the question or completes the statement. *PRINT THE LETTER OF THE CORRECT ANSWER IN THE SPACE AT THE RIGHT.*

1. A certain coordinator does not compliment members of his staff when they come up with good ideas. He feels that coming up with good ideas is part of the job and does not merit special attention.
   This coordinator's practice is

   A. *poor,* because recognition for good ideas is a good motivator
   B. *poor,* because the staff will suspect that the coordinator has no good ideas of his own
   C. *good,* because it is reasonable to assume that employees will tell their supervisor of ways to improve office practice
   D. *good,* because the other members of the staff are not made to seem inferior by comparison

   1.____

2. An employee under your supervision complains about a decision you have made in assigning work in the office. You consider the matter to be unimportant, but it seems to be very important to him. He is excited and very angry.
   Of the following, the MOST appropriate action for you to take FIRST is to

   A. listen to the details of his complaint
   B. refer him to your superior
   C. tell him to *cool off* before discussing the matter
   D. tell him to settle it with the other employees

   2.____

3. An experienced employee complains to his unit supervisor that the latter's continual, very close supervision of his work is unnecessary and annoying. The unit supervisor has been recently appointed.
   Of the following, it would generally be BEST for the unit supervisor to

   A. agree to discontinue all supervision if the employee will agree, if he has any problems, to consult the supervisor
   B. assure the employee that close supervision is necessary but should not be taken personally
   C. consider with the employee what aspects of the supervision could be reduced
   D. explain that he is supervising closely only until he learns what the job is all about

   3.____

4. A coordinator had a clerk assigned to help him review records. One day the coordinator asked the clerk to continue checking the records, and the clerk said, *No, I'm not doing any more of that today.*
   In this instance, the coordinator should IMMEDIATELY

   A. ask the clerk why he will not check the records
   B. ask another clerk to do the job
   C. tell the clerk he must do it or be transferred
   D. contact his own supervisor

   4.____

5. Assume that you have been assigned to supervise other employees. You find that one of your subordinates makes many mistakes whenever he prepares a particular report. Of the following, the MOST desirable course of action for you to follow FIRST in such a situation is to

   A. retrain the subordinate in the preparation of the report
   B. transfer the subordinate to another unit
   C. tell the subordinate to improve or resign
   D. give the employee different duties

6. Some employees of a department have sent an anonymous letter containing many complaints to the department head. Of the following, what is this MOST likely to show about the department?

   A. It is probably a good place to work.
   B. Communications are probably poor.
   C. The complaints are probably unjustified.
   D. These employees are probably untrustworthy.

7. Of the following, the BEST reason for rotating employee work assignments is that such rotation

   A. challenges the ingenuity of supervisors in making assignments
   B. gives each employee a chance at both desirable and undesirable assignments
   C. creates specialists among all employees
   D. increases the competitive spirit among employees

8. A citizen was angry about a parking ticket which he had received, and he insisted on talking to a coordinator about a hearing. The coordinator spoke to him and explained the rules and procedures relating to the disposition of summonses for parking violations. The citizen remained angry and dissatisfied. The coordinator then appealed to the citizen's civic responsibility and asked him if he wished to be an obstructionist. This last action was incorrect.
   How should the coordinator have handled this situation?

   A. Summoned a supervisor immediately and not talked with the angry citizen
   B. Been more sympathetic and shown some agreement with the citizen's complaint
   C. Limited himself to explaining the rules and regulations
   D. Shown some anger himself in order to reduce the citizen's anger

9. A coordinator has had several problems with a clerk who assists him. He calls the clerk in for a discussion of the matters.
   Which of the following should comprise the MAJOR part of the discussion?

   A. All the things the clerk has done wrong
   B. The most recent things the clerk has done wrong
   C. The things the clerk has done well in addition to the things he has done wrong
   D. The clerk's previous experience and personal problems

Questions 10-14.

DIRECTIONS: Questions 10 through 14 are to be answered SOLELY on the basis of the following passage.

The laws with which criminal courts are concerned contain threats of punishment for infraction of specified rules. Consequently, the courts are organized primarily for implementation of the punitive societal reaction of crime. While the informal organization of most courts allows the judge to use discretion as to which guilty persons actually are to be punished, the threat of punishment for all guilty persons always is present. Also, in recent years a number of formal provisions for the use of non-punitive and treatment methods by the criminal courts have been made, but the threat of punishment remains, even for the recipients of the treatment and non-punitive measures. For example, it has become possible for courts to grant probation, which can be non-punitive, to some offenders, but the probationer is constantly under the threat of punishment, for, if he does not maintain the conditions of his probation, he may be imprisoned. As the treatment reaction to crime becomes more popular, the criminal courts may have as their sole function the determination of the guilt or innocence of the accused persons, leaving the problem of correcting criminals entirely to outsiders. Under such conditions, the organization of the court system, the duties and activities of court personnel, and the nature of the trial all would be decidedly different.

10. Which one of the following is the BEST description of the subject matter of the above passage?
The

    A. value of non-punitive measures for criminals
    B. effect of punishment on guilty individuals
    C. punitive functions of the criminal courts
    D. success of probation as a deterrent of crime

11. It may be INFERRED from the above passage that the present traditional organization of the criminal court system is a result of

    A. the nature of the laws with which these courts are concerned
    B. a shift from non-punitive to punitive measures for correctional purposes
    C. an informal arrangement between court personnel and the government
    D. a formal decision made by court personnel to increase efficiency

12. All persons guilty of breaking certain specified rules, according to the above passage, are subject to the threat of

    A. treatment   B. punishment
    C. probation   D. retrial

13. According to the above passage, the decision whether or not to punish a guilty person is a function USUALLY performed by

    A. the jury   B. the criminal code
    C. the judge   D. corrections personnel

14. According to the above passage, which one of the following is a possible effect of an increase in the *treatment reactions to crime?* 14.____

    A. A decrease in the number of court personnel
    B. An increase in the number of criminal trials
    C. Less reliance on probation as a non-punitive treatment measure
    D. A decrease in the functions of the court following determination of guilt

15. Which of the following actions would usually be MOST appropriate for a coordinator to take after receiving an instruction sheet from his supervisor explaining a new procedure which is to be followed? 15.____

    A. Put the instruction sheet aside temporarily until he determines what is wrong with the old procedure
    B. Call his supervisor and ask if the procedure is one he must implement immediately
    C. Write a memorandum to the supervisor asking for more details
    D. Try the new procedure and advise the supervisor of any problem or possible improvements

16. Assume that you are in charge of an office handling a large volume of various types of clerical work. 16.____
    The one of the following that must be done FIRST to promote even distribution and proper flow of work is to determine

    A. when additional work will come to the office
    B. the capabilities of the staff
    C. the type of tasks to be done and their priorities
    D. the time required for each task

17. In a miscellaneous correspondence folder in a file drawer, it is usually MOST helpful if letters are arranged according to 17.____

    A. date with the most recent date on the bottom
    B. date with the most recent date on the top
    C. subject with the subjects alphabetically arranged
    D. name with the names arranged geographically

18. Of the following, which one is considered the PRIMARY advantage of using a committee to resolve a problem in an organization? 18.____

    A. No one person will be held accountable for the decision since a group of people was involved
    B. People with different backgrounds give attention to the problem
    C. The decision will take considerable time so there is unlikely to be a decision that will later be regretted
    D. One person cannot dominate the decision-making process

19. Assume that as a coordinator you have been asked to redesign a form used in your office. 19.____
    Of the following, your MOST important consideration should be the

    A. sequence of items on the form
    B. number of items to be included on the form
    C. number of copies that are required
    D. purpose of the form

20. Employees in a certain office come to their supervisor with all their complaints about the office and the work. Almost every employee has had at least one minor complaint at some time.
The situation with respect to complaints in this office may BEST be described as probably

   A. *good;* employees who complain care about their jobs and work hard
   B. *good;* grievances brought out into the open can be corrected
   C. *bad;* only serious complaints should be discussed
   D. *bad;* it indicates the staff does not have confidence in the administration

KEY (CORRECT ANSWERS)

1. A
2. A
3. C
4. A
5. A

6. B
7. B
8. C
9. C
10. C

11. A
12. B
13. C
14. D
15. D

16. C
17. B
18. B
19. D
20. B

EXAMINATION SECTION
TEST 1

DIRECTIONS: Each question or incomplete statement is followed by several suggested answers or completions. Select the one that BEST answers the question or completes the statement. *PRINT THE LETTER OF THE CORRECT ANSWER IN THE SPACE AT THE RIGHT.*

1. In public agencies, communications should be based PRIMARILY on a
   A. two-way flow from the top down and from the bottom up, most of which should be given in writing to avoid ambiguity
   B. multi-direction flow among all levels and with outside persons
   C. rapid, internal one-way flow from the top down
   D. two-way flow of information, most of which should be given orally for purposes of clarity

   1.____

2. In some organizations, changes in policy or procedures are often communicated by word of mouth from supervisors to employees with no prior discussion or exchange of viewpoints with employees.
   This procedure often produces employee dissatisfaction CHIEFLY because
   A. information is mostly unusable since a considerable amount of time is required to transmit information
   B. lower-level supervisors tend to be excessively concerned with minor details
   C. management has failed to seek employees' advice before making changes
   D. valuable staff time is lost between decision-making and the implementation of decisions

   2.____

3. For good letter writing, you should try to visualize the person to whom you are writing, especially if you know him.
   Of the following rules, it is LEAST helpful in such visualization to think of
   A. the person's likes and dislikes, his concerns, and his needs
   B. what you would be likely to say if speaking in person
   C. what you would expect to be asked if speaking in person
   D. your official position in order to be certain that your words are proper

   3.____

4. One approach to good informal letter writing is to make letters and conversational.
   All of the following practices will usually help to do this EXCEPT:
   A. If possible, use a style which is similar to the style used when speaking
   B. Substitute phrases for single words (e.g., *at the present time* for *now*)
   C. Use contractions of words (e.g., *you're* for *you are*)
   D. Use ordinary vocabulary when possible

   4.____

5. All of the following rules will aid in producing clarity in report-writing EXCEPT:
   A. Give specific details or examples, if possible
   B. Keep related words close together in each sentence
   C. Present information in sequential order
   D. Put several thoughts or ideas in each paragraph

6. The one of the following statements about public relations which is MOST accurate is that
   A. in the long run, appearance gains better results than performance
   B. objectivity is decreased if outside public relations consultants are employed
   C. public relations is the responsibility of every employee
   D. public relations should be based on a formal publicity program

7. The form of communication which is usually considered to be MOST personally directed to the intended recipient is the
   A. brochure   B. film   C. letter   D. radio

8. In general, a document that presents an organization's views or opinions on a particular topic is MOST accurately known as a
   A. tear sheet
   B. position paper
   C. flyer
   D. journal

9. Assume that you have been asked to speak before an organization of persons who oppose a newly announced program in which you are involved. You feel tense about talking to this group.
   Which of the following rules generally would be MOST useful in gaining rapport when speaking before the audience?
   A. Impress them with your experience
   B. Stress all areas of disagreement
   C. Talk to the group as to one person
   D. Use formal grammar and language

10. An organization must have an effective public relations program since, at its best, public relations is a bridge to change.
    All of the following statements about communication and human behavior have validity EXCEPT:
    A. People are more likely to talk about controversial matters with like-minded people than with those holding other views
    B. The earlier an experience, the more powerful its effect since it influences how later experiences will be interpreted
    C. In periods of social tension, official sources gain increased believability
    D. Those who are already interested in a topic are the ones who are most open to receive new communications about it

11. An employee should be encouraged to talk easily and frankly when he is dealing with his supervisor.
    In order to encourage such free communication, it would be MOST appropriate for a supervisor to behave in a(n)
    A. sincere manner; assure the employee that you will deal with him honestly and openly
    B. official manner; you are a supervisor and must always act formally with subordinates
    C. investigative manner; you must probe and question to get to a basis of trust
    D. unemotional manner; the employee's emotions and background should play no part in your dealings with him

12. Research findings show that an increase in free communication within an agency GENERALLY results in which one of the following?
    A. Improved morale and productivity
    B. Increased promotional opportunities
    C. An increase in authority
    D. A spirit of honesty

13. Assume that you are a supervisor and your superiors have given you a new-type procedure to be followed.
    Before passing this information on to your subordinates, the one of the following actions that you should take FIRST is to
    A. ask your superiors to send out a memorandum to the entire staff
    B. clarify the procedure in your own mind
    C. set up a training course to provide instruction on the new procedure
    D. write a memorandum to your subordinates

14. Communication is necessary for an organization to be effective.
    The one of the following which is LEAST important for most communication systems is that
    A. messages are sent quickly and directly to the person who needs them to operate
    B. information should be conveyed understandably and accurately
    C. the method used to transmit information should be kept secret so that security can be maintained
    D. senders of messages must know how their messages are received and acted upon

15. Which one of the following is the CHIEF advantage of listening willingly to subordinates and encouraging them to talk freely and honestly?
    It
    A. reveals to supervisors the degree to which ideas that are passed down are accepted by subordinates
    B. reduces the participation of subordinates in the operation of the department
    C. encourages subordinates to try for promotion
    D. enables supervisors to learn more readily what the *grapevine* is saying

16. A supervisor may be informed through either oral or written reports. 16.____
Which one of the following is an ADVANTAGE of using oral reports?
    A. There is no need for a formal record of the report.
    B. An exact duplicate of the report is not easily transmitted to others.
    C. A good oral report requires little time for preparation.
    D. An oral report involves two-way communication between a subordinate and his supervisor.

17. Of the following, the MOST important reason why supervisors should 17.____
communicate effectively with the public is to
    A. improve the public's understanding of information that is important for them to know
    B. establish a friendly relationship
    C. obtain information about the kinds of people who come to the agency
    D. convince the public that services are adequate

18. Supervisors should generally NOT use phrases like *too hard*, *too easy*, and 18.____
a lot PRINCIPALLY because such phrases
    A. may be offensive to some minority groups
    B. are too informal
    C. mean different things to different people
    D. are difficult to remember

19. The ability to communicate clearly and concisely is an important element in 19.____
effective leadership.
Which of the following statements about oral and written communication is GENERALLY true?
    A. Oral communication is more time-consuming.
    B. Written communication is more likely to be misinterpreted.
    C. Oral communication is useful only in emergencies.
    D. Written communication is useful mainly when giving information to fewer than twenty people.

20. Rumors can often have harmful and disruptive effects on an organization. 20.____
Which one of the following is the BEST way to prevent rumors from becoming a problem?
    A. Refuse to act on rumors, thereby making them less believable.
    B. Increase the amount of information passed along by the *grapevine*.
    C. Distribute as much factual information as possible.
    D. Provide training in report writing.

21. Suppose that a subordinate asks you about a rumor he has heard. The rumor 21.____
deals with a subject which your superiors consider *confidential*.
Which of the following BEST describes how you should answer the subordinate? Tell

A. the subordinate that you don't make the rules and that he should speak to higher ranking officials
B. the subordinate that you will ask your superior for information
C. him only that you cannot comment on the matter
D. him the rumor is not true

22. Supervisors often find it difficult to *get their message across* when instructing newly appointed employees in their various duties.
The MAIN reason for this is generally that the
    A. duties of the employees have increased
    B. supervisor is often so expert in his area that he fails to see it from the learner's point of view
    C. supervisor adapts his instruction to the slowest learner in the group
    D. new employees are younger, less concerned with job security and more interested in fringe benefits

23. Assume that you are discussing a job problem with an employee under your supervision. During the discussion, you see that the man's eyes are turning away from you and that he is not paying attention.
In order to get the man's attention, you should FIRST
    A. ask him to look you in the eye
    B. talk to him about sports
    C. tell him he is being very rude
    D. change your tone of voice

24. As a supervisor, you may find it necessary to conduct meetings with your subordinates.
Of the following, which would be MOST helpful in assuring that a meeting accomplishes the purpose for which it was called?
    A. Give notice of the conclusions you would like to reach at the start of the meeting.
    B. Delay the start of the meeting until everyone is present.
    C. Write down points to be discussed in proper sequence.
    D. Make sure everyone is clear on whatever conclusions have been reached and on what must be done after the meeting.

25. Every supervisor will occasionally be called upon to deliver a reprimand to a subordinate. If done properly, this can greatly help an employee improve his performance.
Which one of the following is NOT a good practice to follow when giving a reprimand?
    A. Maintain your composure and temper
    B. Reprimand a subordinate in the presence of other employees so they can learn the same lesson
    C. Try to understand why the employee was not able to perform satisfactorily
    D. Let your knowledge of the man involved determine the exact nature of the reprimand

KEY (CORRECT ANSWERS)

1.	C	11.	A
2.	B	12.	A
3.	D	13.	B
4.	B	14.	C
5.	D	15.	A
6.	C	16.	D
7.	C	17.	A
8.	B	18.	C
9.	C	19.	B
10.	C	20.	C

21.	B
22.	B
23.	D
24.	D
25.	B

TEST 2

DIRECTIONS: Each question or incomplete statement is followed by several suggested answers or completions. Select the one that BEST answers the question or completes the statement. *PRINT THE LETTER OF THE CORRECT ANSWER IN THE SPACE AT THE RIGHT.*

1. Usually one thinks of communication as a single step, essentially that of transmitting an idea.
   Actually, however, this is only part of a total process, the FIRST step of which should be
   A. the prompt dissemination of the idea to those who may be affected by it
   B. motivating those affected to take the required action
   C. clarifying the idea in one's own mind
   D. deciding to whom the idea is to be communicated

   1.____

2. Research studies on patterns of informal communication have concluded that most individuals in a group tend to be passive recipients of news, while a few make it their business to spread it around in an organization.
   With this conclusion in mind, it would be MOST correct for the supervisor to attempt to identify these few individuals and
   A. give them the complete facts on important matters in advance of others
   B. inform the other subordinates of the identity of these few individuals so that their influence may be minimized
   C. keep them straight on the facts on important matters
   D. warn them to cease passing along any information to others

   2.____

3. The one of the following which is the PRINCIPAL advantage of making an oral report is that it
   A. affords an immediate opportunity for two-way communication between the subordinate and superior
   B. is an easy method for the superior to use in transmitting information to others of equal rank
   C. saves the time of all concerned
   D. permits more precise pinpointing of praise or blame by means of follow-up questions by the superior

   3.____

4. An agency may sometimes undertake a public relations program of a defensive nature.
   With reference to the use of defensive public relations, it would be MOST correct to state that it
   A. is bound to be ineffective since defensive statements, even though supported by factual data, can never hope to even partly overcome the effects of prior unfavorable attacks
   B. proves that the agency has failed to establish good relationships with newspapers, radio stations, or other means of publicity

   4.____

C. shows that the upper echelons of the agency have failed to develop sound public relations procedures and techniques
D. is sometimes required to aid morale by protecting the agency from unjustified criticism and misunderstanding of policies or procedures

5. Of the following factors which contribute to possible undesirable public attitudes towards an agency, the one which is MOST susceptible to being changed by the efforts of the individual employee in an organization is that
   A. enforcement of unpopular regulations as offended many individuals
   B. the organization itself has an unsatisfactory reputation
   C. the public is not interested in agency matters
   D. there are many errors in judgment committed by individual subordinates

6. It is not enough for an agency's services to be of a high quality; attention must also be given to the acceptability of these services to the general public.
   This statement is GENERALLY
   A. *false*; a superior quality of service automatically wins public support
   B. *true*; the agency cannot generally progress beyond the understanding and support of the public
   C. *false*; the acceptance by the public of agency services determines their quality
   D. *true*; the agency is generally unable to engage in any effective enforcement activity without public support

7. Sustained agency participation in a program sponsored by a community organization is MOST justified when
   A. the achievement of agency objectives in some area depends partly on the activity of this organization
   B. the community organization is attempting to widen the base of participation in all community affairs
   C. the agency is uncertain as to what the community wants
   D. the agency is uncertain as to what the community wants

8. Of the following, the LEAST likely way in which a records system may serve a supervisor is in
   A. developing a sympathetic and cooperative public attitude toward the agency
   B. improving the quality of supervision by permitting a check on the accomplishment of subordinates
   C. permit a precise prediction of the exact incidences in specific categories for the following year
   D. helping to take the guesswork out of the distribution of the agency

9. Assuming that the *grapevine* in any organization is virtually indestructible, the one of the following which it is MOST important for management to understand is:
   A. What is being spread by means of the *grapevine* and the reason for spreading it
   B. What is being spread by means of the *grapevine* and how it is being spread
   C. Who is involved in spreading the information that is on the *grapevine*
   D. Why those who are involved in spreading the information are doing so

10. When the supervisor writes a report concerning an investigation to which he has been assigned, it should be LEAST intended to provide
    A. a permanent official record of relevant information gathered
    B. a summary of case findings limited to facts which tend to indicate the guilt of a suspect
    C. a statement of the facts on which higher authorities may base a corrective or disciplinary action
    D. other investigators with information so that they may continue with other phases of the investigation

11. In survey work, questionnaires rather than interviews are sometimes used. The one of the following which is a DISADVANTAGE of the questionnaire method as compared with the interview is the
    A. difficulty of accurately interpreting the results
    B. problem of maintaining anonymity of the participant
    C. fact that it is relatively uneconomical
    D. requirement of special training for the distribution of questionnaires

12. In his contacts with the public, an employee should attempt to create a good climate of support for his agency.
    This statement is GENERALLY
    A. *false*; such attempts are clearly beyond the scope of his responsibility
    B. *true*; employees of an agency who come in contact with the public have the opportunity to affect public relations
    C. *false*; such activity should be restricted to supervisors trained in public relations techniques
    D. *true*; the future expansion of the agency depends to a great extent on continued public support of the agency

13. The repeated use by a supervisor of a call for volunteers to get a job done is objectionable MAINLY because it
    A. may create a feeling of animosity between the volunteers and the non-volunteers
    B. may indicate that the supervisor is avoiding responsibility for making assignments which will be most productive
    C. is an indication that the supervisor is not familiar with the individual capabilities of his men
    D. is unfair to men who, for valid reasons, do not, or cannot volunteer

14. Of the following statements concerning subordinates' expressions to a supervisor of their opinions and feelings concerning work situations, the one which is MOST correct is that
    A. by listening and responding to such expressions the supervisor encourages the development of complaints
    B. the lack of such expressions should indicate to the supervisor that there is a high level of job satisfaction
    C. the more the supervisor listens to and responds to such expressions, the more he demonstrates lack of supervisory ability
    D. by listening and responding to such expressions, the supervisor will enable many subordinates to understand and solve their own problems on the job

15. In attempting to motivate employees, rewards are considered preferable to punishment PRIMARILY because
    A. punishment seldom has any effect on human behavior
    B. punishment usually results in decreased production
    C. supervisors find it difficult to punish
    D. rewards are more likely to result in willing cooperation

16. In an attempt to combat the low morale in his organization, a high level supervisor publicized an *open-door policy* to allow employees who wished to do so to come to him with their complaints.
    Which of the following is LEAST likely to account for the fact that no employee came in with a complaint?
    A. Employees are generally reluctant to go over the heads of their immediate supervisor.
    B. The employees did not feel that management would help them.
    C. The low morale was not due to complaints associated with the job.
    D. The employees felt that they had more to lose than to gain.

17. It is MOST desirable to use written instructions rather than oral instructions for a particular job when
    A. a mistake on the job will not be serious
    B. the job can be completed in a short time
    C. there is no need to explain the job minutely
    D. the job involves many details

18. If you receive a telephone call regarding a matter which your office does not handle, you should FIRST
    A. give the caller the telephone number of the proper office so that he can dial again
    B. offer to transfer the caller to the proper office
    C. suggest that the caller re-dial since he probably dialed incorrectly
    D. tell the caller he has reached the wrong office and then hang up

19. When you answer the telephone, the MOST important reason for identifying yourself and your organization is to
    A. give the caller time to collect his or her thoughts
    B. impress the caller with your courtesy
    C. inform the caller that he or she has reached the right number
    D. set a business-like tone at the beginning of the conversation

20. As soon as you pick up the phone, a very angry caller begins immediately to complain about city agencies and *red tape*. He says that he has been shifted to two or three different offices. It turs out that he is seeking information which is not immediately available to you. You believe, you know, however, where it can be found.
    Which of the following actions is the BEST one for you to take?
    A. To eliminate all confusion, suggest that the caller write the agency stating explicitly what he wants.
    B. Apologize by telling the caller how busy city agencies now are, but also tell him directly that you do not have the information he needs.
    C. Ask for the caller's telephone number and assure him you will call back after you have checked further.
    D. Give the caller the name and telephone number of the person who might be able to help, but explain that you are not positive he will get results/

21. Which of the following approaches usually provides the BEST communication in the objectives and values of a new program which is to be introduced?
    A. A general written description of the program by the program manager for review by those who share responsibility
    B. An effective verbal presentation by the program manager to those affected
    C. Development of the plan and operational approach in carrying out the program by the program manager assisted by his key subordinates
    D. Development of the plan by the program manager's supervisor

22. What is the BEST approach for introducing change?
    A
    A. combination of written and also verbal communication to all personnel affected by the change
    B. general bulletin to all personnel
    C. meeting pointing out all the values of the new approach
    D. written directive to key personnel

23. Of the following, committees are BEST used for
    A. advising the head of the organization
    B. improving functional work
    C. making executive decisions
    D. making specific planning decisions

24. An effective discussion leader is one who   24._____
    A. announces the problem and his preconceived solution at the start of the discussion
    B. guides and directs the discussion according to pre-arranged outline
    C. interrupts or corrects confused participants to save time
    D. permits anyone to say anything at any time

25. The human relations movement in management theory is basically concerned with   25._____
    A. counteracting employee unrest
    B. eliminating the *time and motion* man
    C. interrelationships among individuals in organizations
    D. the psychology of the worker

KEY (CORRECT ANSWERS)

1.	C	11.	A
2.	C	12.	B
3.	A	13.	B
4.	D	14.	D
5.	D	15.	D
6.	B	16.	C
7.	A	17.	D
8.	C	18.	B
9.	A	19.	C
10.	B	20.	C

21.	C
22.	A
23.	A
24.	B
25.	C

COMMUNICATION

EXAMINATION SECTION
TEST 1

DIRECTIONS: Each question or incomplete statement is followed by several suggested answers or completions. Select the one that BEST answers the question or completes the statement. *PRINT THE LETTER OF THE CORRECT ANSWER IN THE SPACE AT THE RIGHT.*

1. In some agencies the counsel to the agency head is given the right to bypass the chain of command and issue orders directly to the staff concerning matters that involve certain specific processes and practices.
   This situation MOST nearly illustrates the principle of _____ authority.
   A. the acceptance theory of
   B. multiple-linear
   C. splintered
   D. functional

2. It is commonly understood that communication is an important part of the administrative process.
   Which of the following is NOT a valid principle of the communication process in administration?
   A. The channels of communication should be spontaneous.
   B. The lines of communication should be as direct and as short as possible.
   C. Communications should be authenticated.
   D. The persons serving in communications centers should be competent.

3. Of the following, the one factor which is generally considered LEAST essential to successful committee operations is
   A. stating a clear definition of the authority and scope of the committee
   B. selecting the committee chairman carefully
   C. limiting the size of the committee to four persons
   D. limiting the subject matter to that which can be handled in group discussion

4. Of the following, the failure by line managers to accept and appreciate the benefits and limitations of a new program or system VERY FREQUENTLY can be traced to the
   A. budgetary problems involved
   B. resultant need to reduce staff
   C. lack of controls it engenders
   D. failure of top management to support its implementation

5. If a manager were thinking about using a committee of subordinates to solve an operating problem, which of the following would generally NOT be an advantage of such use of the committee approach?
   A. Improved coordination
   B. Low cost
   C. Increased motivation
   D. Integrated judgment

6. Every supervisor has many occasions to lead a conference or participate in a conference of some sort.
Of the following statements that pertain to conferences and conference leadership, which is generally considered to be MOST valid?
   A. Since World War II, the trend has been toward fewer shared decisions and more conferences.
   B. The most important part of a conference leader's job is to direct discussion.
   C. In providing opportunities for group interaction, management should avoid consideration of its past management philosophy.
   D. A good administrator cannot lead a good conference if he is a poor public speaker.

7. Of the following, it is usually LEAST desirable for a conference leader to
   A. call the name of a person after asking a question
   B. summarize proceedings periodically
   C. make a practice of repeating questions
   D. ask a question without indicating who is to reply

8. Assume that, in a certain organization, a situation has developed in which there is little difference in status or authority between individuals.
Which of the following would be the MOST likely result with regard to communication in this organization?
   A. Both the accuracy and flow of communication will be improved.
   B. Both the accuracy and flow of communication will substantially decrease.
   C. Employees will seek more formal lines of communication.
   D. Neither the flow nor the accuracy of communication will be improved over the former hierarchical structure.

9. The main function of many agency administrative officers is "information management." Information that is received by an administrative officer may be classified as active or passive, depending upon whether or not it requires the recipient to take some action.
Of the following, the item received which is clearly the MOST active information is
   A. an appointment of a new staff member
   B. a payment voucher for a new desk
   C. a press release concerning a past event
   D. the minutes of a staff meeting

10. Of the following, the one LEAST considered to be a communication barrier is
    A. group feedback
    B. charged words
    C. selective perception
    D. symbolic meanings

11. Management studies support the hypothesis that, in spite of the tendency of employees to censor the information communicated to their supervisor, subordinates are more likely to communicate problem-oriented information UPWARD when they have a
    A. long period of service in the organization
    B. high degree of trust in the supervisor
    C. high educational level
    D. low status on the organizational ladder

11.____

12. Electronic data processing equipment can produce more information faster than can be generated by any other means.
    In view of this, the MOST important problem faced by management at present is to
    A. keep computers fully occupied
    B. find enough computer personnel
    C. assimilate and properly evaluate the information
    D. obtain funds to establish appropriate information systems

12.____

13. A well-designed management information system essentially provides each executive and manager the information he needs for
    A. determining computer time requirements
    B. planning and measuring results
    C. drawing a new organization chart
    D. developing a new office layout

13.____

14. It is generally agreed that management policies should be periodically reappraised and restated in accordance with current conditions.
    Of the following, the approach which would be MOST effective in determining whether a policy should be revised is to
    A. conduct interviews with staff members at all levels in order to ascertain the relationship between the policy and actual practice
    B. make proposed revisions in the policy and apply it to current problems
    C. make up hypothetical situations using both the old policy and a revised version in order to make comparisons
    D. call a meeting of top level staff in order to discuss ways of revising the policy

14.____

15. Your superior has asked you to notify division employees of an important change in one of the operating procedures described in the division manual. Every employee presently has a copy of this manual.
    Which of the following is normally the MOST practical way to get the employees to understand such a change?
    A. Notify each employee individually of the change and answer any questions he might have
    B. Send a written notice to key personnel, directing them to inform the people under them

15.____

C. Call a general meeting, distribute a corrected page for the manual, and discuss the change
D. Send a memo to employees describing the change in general terms and asking them to make the necessary corrections in their copies of the manual

16. Assume that the work in your department involves the use of any technical terms.
In such a situation, when you are answering inquiries from the general public, it would usually be BEST to
   A. use simple language and avoid the technical terms
   B. employ the technical terms whenever possible
   C. bandy technical terms freely, but explain each term in parentheses
   D. apologize if you are forced to use a technical term

16._____

17. Suppose that you receive a telephone call from someone identifying himself as an employee in another city department who asks to be given information which your own department regards as confidential.
Which of the following is the BEST way of handling such a request?
   A. Give the information requested, since your caller as official standing
   B. Grant the request, provided the caller gives you a signed receipt
   C. Refuse the request, because you have no way of knowing whether the caller is really who he claims to be
   D. Explain that the information is confidential and inform the caller of the channels he must go through to have the information released to him

17._____

18. Studies show that office employees place high importance on the social and human aspects of the organization. What office employees like best about their jobs is the kind of people with whom they work. So strive hard to group people who are most likely to get along well together.
Based on this information, it is MOST reasonable to assume that office workers are most pleased to work in a group which
   A. is congenial   B. has high productivity
   C. allows individual creativity   D. is unlike other groups

18._____

19. A certain supervisor does not compliment members of his staff when they come up with good ideas. He feels that coming up with good ideas is part of the job and does not merit special attention.
This supervisor's practice is
   A. *poor*, because recognition for good ideas is a good motivator
   B. *poor*, because the staff will suspect that the supervisor has no good ideas of his own
   C. *good*, because it is reasonable to assume that employees will tell their supervisor of ways to improve office practice
   D. *good*, because the other members of the staff are not made to seem inferior by comparison

19._____

20. Some employees of a department have sent an anonymous letter containing many complaints to the department head.
Of the following, what is this MOST likely to show about the department?
    A. It is probably a good place to work.
    B. Communications are probably poor.
    C. The complaints are probably unjustified.
    D. These employees are probably untrustworthy.

21. Which of the following actions would usually be MOST appropriate for a supervisor to take after receiving an instruction sheet from his superior explaining a new procedure which is to be followed?
    A. Put the instruction sheet aside temporarily until he determines what is wrong with the old procedure.
    B. Call his superior and ask whether the procedure is one he must implement immediately.
    C. Write a memorandum to the superior asking for more details.
    D. Try the new procedure and advise the superior of any problems or possible improvements.

22. Of the following, which one is considered the PRIMARY advantage of using a committee to resolved a problem in an organization?
    A. No one person will be held accountable for the decision since a group of people was involved.
    B. People with different backgrounds give attention to the problem.
    C. The decision will take considerable time so there is unlikely to be a decision that will later be regretted.
    D. One person cannot dominate the decision-making process.

23. Employees in a certain office come to their supervisor with all their complaints about the office and the work. Almost every employee has had at least one minor complaint at some time.
The situation with respect to complaints in this office may BEST be described as probably
    A. *good*; employees who complain care about their jobs and work hard
    B. *good*; grievances brought out into the open can be corrected
    C. *bad*; only serious complaints should be discussed
    D. *bad*; it indicates the staff does not have confidence in the administration

24. The administrator who allows his staff to suggest ways to do their work will usually find that
    A. this practice contributes to high productivity
    B. the administrator's ideas produce greater output
    C. clerical employees suggest inefficient work methods
    D. subordinate employees resent performing a management function

25. The MAIN purpose for a supervisor's questioning the employees at a conference he is holding is to 25.____
    A. stress those areas of information covered but not understood by the participants
    B. encourage participants to think through the problem under discussion
    C. catch those subordinates who are not paying attention
    D. permit the more knowledgeable participants to display their grasp of the problems being discussed

KEY (CORRECT ANSWERS)

1.	D		11.	B
2.	A		12.	C
3.	C		13.	B
4.	D		14.	A
5.	B		15.	C
6.	B		16.	A
7.	C		17.	D
8.	D		18.	A
9.	A		19.	A
10.	A		20.	B

21. D
22. B
23. B
24. A
25. B

TEST 2

DIRECTIONS: Each question or incomplete statement is followed by several suggested answers or completions. Select the one that BEST answers the question or completes the statement. *PRINT THE LETTER OF THE CORRECT ANSWER IN THE SPACE AT THE RIGHT.*

1. For a superior to use *consultative supervision* with his subordinates effectively, it is ESSENTIAL that he
    A. accept the fact that his formal authority will be weakened by the procedure
    B. admit that he does not know more than all his men together and that his ideas are not always best
    C. utilize a committee system so that the procedure is orderly
    D. make sure that all subordinates are consulted so that no one feels left out

1.____

2. The *grapevine* is an informal means of communication in an organization. The attitude of a supervisor with respect to the grapevine should be to
    A. ignore it since it deals mainly with rumors and sensational information
    B. regard it as a serious danger which should be eliminated
    C. accept it as a real line of communication which should be listened to
    D. utilize it for most purposes instead of the official line of communication

2.____

3. The supervisor of an office that must deal with the public should realize that planning in this type of work situation
    A. is useless because he does not know how many people will request service or what service they will request
    B. must be done at a higher level but that he should be ready to implement the results of such planning
    C. is useful primarily for those activities that are not concerned with public contact
    D. is useful for all the activities of the office, including those that relate to public contact

3.____

4. Assume that it is your job to receive incoming telephone calls. Those calls which you cannot handle yourself have to be transferred to the appropriate office.
   If you receive an outside call for an extension line which is busy, the one of the following which you should do FIRST is to
    A. interrupt the person speaking on the extension and tell him a call is waiting
    B. tell the caller the line is busy and let him know every thirty seconds whether or not it is free
    C. leave the caller on "hold" until the extension is free
    D. tell the caller the line is busy and ask him if he wishes to wait

4.____

5. Your superior has subscribed to several publications directly related to your division's work, and he has asked you to see to it that the publications are circulated among the supervisory personnel in the division. There are eight supervisors involved.
The BEST method of insuring that all eight see these publications is to
   A. place the publication in the division's general reference library as soon as it arrives
   B. inform each supervisor whenever a publication arrives and remind all of them that they are responsible for reading it
   C. prepare a standard slip that can be stapled to each publication, listing the eight supervisors and saying, "Please read, initial your name, and pass along"
   D. send a memo to the eight supervisors saying that they may wish to purchase individual subscriptions in their own names if they are interested in seeing each issue

6. Your superior has telephoned a number of key officials in your agency to ask whether they can meet at a certain time next month. He has found that they can all make it, and he has asked you to confirm the meeting.
Which of the following is the BEST way to confirm such a meeting?
   A. Note the meeting on your superior's calendar.
   B. Post a notice of the meeting on the agency bulletin board.
   C. Call the officials on the day of the meeting to remind them of the meeting.
   D. Write a memo to each official involved, repeating the time and place of the meeting.

7. Assume that a new city regulation requires that certain kinds of private organizations file information forms with your department. You have been asked to write the short explanatory message that will be printed on the front cover of the pamphlet containing the forms and instructions.
Which of the following would be the MOST appropriate way of beginning this message?
   A. Get the readers' attention by emphasizing immediately that there are legal penalties for organizations that fail to file before a certain date.
   B. Briefly state the nature of the enclosed forms and the types of organizations that must file.
   C. Say that your department is very sorry to have to put organizations to such an inconvenience.
   D. Quote the entire regulation adopted by the city, even if it is quite long and is expressed din complicated legal language.

8. Suppose that you have been told to make up the vacation schedule for the 18 employees in a particular unit. In order for the unit to operate effectively, only a few employees can be on vacation at the same time.
Which of the following is the MOST advisable approach in making up the schedule?
   A. Draw up a schedule assigning vacations in alphabetical order
   B. Find out when the supervisors want to take their vacations, and randomly assign whatever periods are left to the non-supervisory personnel

C. Assign the most desirable times to employees of longest standing and the least desirable times to the newest employees
D. Have all employees state their own preference, and then work out any conflicts in consultation with the people involved

9. Assume that you have been asked to prepare job descriptions for various positions in your department.
Which of the following are the basic points that should be covered in a *job description*?
   A. General duties and responsibilities of the position, with examples of day-to-day tasks
   B. Comments on the performances of present employees
   C. Estimates of the number of openings that may be available in each category during the coming year
   D. Instructions for carrying out the specific tasks assigned to your department

9._____

10. Of the following, the biggest DISADVANTAGE in allowing a free flow of communications in an agency is that such a free flow
    A. decreases creativity
    B. increases the use of the *grapevine*
    C. lengthens the chain of command
    D. reduces the executive's power to direct the flow of information

10._____

11. A downward flow of authority in an organization is one example of _____ communication.
    A. horizontal   B. informal   C. circular   D. vertical

11._____

12. Of the following, the one that would MOST likely block effective communication is
    A. concentration only on the issues at hand
    B. lack of interest or commitment
    C. use of written reports
    D. use of charts and graphs

12._____

13. An ADVANTAGE of the *lecture* as a teaching tool is that it
    A. enables a person to present his ideas to a large number of people
    B. allows the audience to retain a maximum of the information given
    C. holds the attention of the audience for the longest time
    D. enables the audience member to easily recall the main points

13._____

14. An ADVANTAGE of the *small-group* discussion as a teaching tool is that
    A. it always focuses attention on one person as the leader
    B. it places collective responsibility on the group as a whole
    C. its members gain experience by summarizing the ideas of others
    D. each member of the group acts as a member of a team

14._____

15. The one of the following that is an ADVANTAGE of a *large-group* discussion, when compared to a small-group discussion, is that the large-group discussion
    A. moves along more quickly than a small-group discussion
    B. allows its participants to feel more at ease, and speak out more freely
    C. gives the whole group a chance to exchange ideas on a certain subject at the same occasion
    D. allows its members to feel a greater sense of personal responsibility

KEY (CORRECT ANSWERS)

1.	D	6.	D	11.	D
2.	C	7.	B	12.	B
3.	D	8.	D	13.	A
4.	D	9.	A	14.	D
5.	C	10.	D	15.	C

EXAMINATION SECTION
TEST 1

DIRECTIONS: Each question or incomplete statement is followed by several suggested answers or completions. Select the one that BEST answers the question or completes the statement. *PRINT THE LETTER OF THE CORRECT ANSWER IN THE SPACE AT THE RIGHT.*

1. Managing conflict effectively by avoiding no-win situations, positively influencing the actions of others and using _____ strategies are what make a great leader. 1.____
   A. persuasive   B. ambiguous   C. prosecution   D. performance

2. In today's business world, collaboration will bring together people from distinct backgrounds. These collaborative groups may not share common norms, morals or _____, but they can offer unique _____. 2.____
   A. vocabulary; perspectives   B. salaries; vocabulary
   C. modifications; insights   D. perspectives; salaries

3. E-mail is a great tool for communication; however, which of the following should you be careful of when in electronic communication with a colleague? 3.____
   A. Font size   B. E-mail length
   C. Font color   D. Tone of voice

4. A formal relationship can BEST be described as 4.____
   A. regulated by procedures or directives
   B. personal and relaxed
   C. emotionally distant and very uncomfortable
   D. confusing and unproductive

5. John is in a meeting with his supervisor ad coworkers. He is thinking about what he's going to have for dinner that night when his boss asks him a question. John can repeat back what his supervisor said, but he cannot retain what was said during the meeting.
   This is a classic example of failing to 5.____
   A. focus at work
   B. effectively listen
   C. leave personal plans outside the workplace
   D. care about meetings

6. A person's choice of _____ can directly affect communication. 6.____
   A. clothing   B. food   C. hygiene   D. words

7. Why is it important to relax when communicating with team members? 7.____
   A. Relaxing always means having better ideas.
   B. People will automatically like you more if you are relaxed.

C. If you are nervous, you may talk too quickly and make it hard for others to understand your message or directive.
D. No one likes someone who is always working, so it is important to relax and not work too hard.

8. In order to show you are genuinely interested in what others have to say, you should
   A. tell them how nice they are
   B. repeat what they say back to them
   C. nod and find something to compliment them about
   D. ask questions and seek clarification from them

8.____

9. Jack and James are always arguing with one another. Their supervisor calls each one in separately to talk to them. He asks Jack to think about things from James' point of view and he asks James to do the same for Jack.
   What is the supervisor trying to get each person to do?
   A. Get along   B. Be positive
   C. Communicate effectively D. Empathize

9.____

10. When working in groups, disagreements
    A. should be avoided at all costs
    B. are often a healthy way of building understanding and camaraderie
    C. lead coworkers to hate one another and the company they work for
    D. don't happen if the supervisor chooses the right people to work together

10.____

11. If things go wrong in a group situation, it is important to AVOID
    A. the boss   B. disagreements or arguments
    C. scapegoating   D. being polite and fair to one another

11.____

12. If you are a listener who likes to hear the rationale behind a message, your listening style would be described as _____ style.
    A. results   B. process   C. reasons   D. eye contact

12.____

13. Which of the following BEST describes a psychological barrier in communication?
    A. Molly is so stressed about her paying for her mortgage that she can't focus at work right now.
    B. John doesn't understand a lot of the terms the IT specialist used in an e-mail sent out to everyone.
    C. Jerry is a little older and has a hard time hearing everything so sometimes he misses parts of a conversation.
    D. Linda doesn't want to be at the company for longer than a few months, so she doesn't really try too hard to fit in.

13.____

14. Body language, also known as _____, is really important when building rapport with coworkers and communicating effectively.
    A. verbal language   B. kinesthetic
    C. non-verbal communication D. facial expressions

14.____

15. Which of the following might be a good example of someone who has a "closed" posture?
    A. Hands are apart on the arms of the chair.
    B. His/her arms are folded.
    C. They are directly facing you.
    D. They barely speak above a whisper.

16. Which of the following can eye contact be used for?
    A. To give and receive feedback
    B. To let someone know when it is their turn to speak
    C. To communicate how you feel about someone
    D. All of the above

17. Which of the following is NOT a form of non-verbal communication?
    A. Crossing your arms when talking to someone
    B. Using space within the room in a conversation
    C. Clearing your throat before you speak]
    D. Saying "10-4" when asked if you understand

18. Your best friend has just been hired at the company you work for. You notice he has come into work on several occasions after staying out late the night before. His work has not suffered yet, but you fear it will.
    Which of the following actions should you take to help prevent future problems?
    A. Do nothing; he's your friend but it is his life
    B. Try to talk to him and help him see the importance of not creating bad habits.
    C. Talk to your supervisor and tell him your friend isn't suitable for the job
    D. Tell your friend to change his ways or to quit

19. Interacting with coworkers can be positively or negatively affected by _____ when someone's previous biases and assumptions shape their reactions in future situations.
    A. racism
    B. past experience
    C. interpersonal skills
    D. active listening

20. Which of the following scenarios BEST describes a person who is being subjective?
    A. Sally is fair and honest when she listens to coworkers. She does not take sides and wants the best solution to the problem.
    B. Mike doesn't like Steve, because he thinks Steve is only out for himself. Still, Steve offers valuable insights, so Mike tries not to let personal feelings get in the way of working together.
    C. Jamie is dating Veronica's ex and Veronica just found out. Now, Veronica immediately shoots down anything Jamie suggests during a meeting as irrational and superfluous.
    D. None of the above

21. Which important communications tem is MOST closely defined as "the quality of a sound governed by the rate of vibrations producing it; the degree of highness or lowness of a tone"?
    A. Tone
    B. Pitch
    C. Effective communication
    D. Rationalization

22. _____ is when a person tries to make an imprudent and reckless action seem reasonable.
    A. Projection
    B. Self-deception
    C. Past experience
    D. Rationalization

23. When holding conversations with coworkers, you should
    A. do most of the talking
    B. let others do most of the talking
    C. try to split time between talking and listening
    D. zone out and wait for the meeting to finish

24. A new hire just arrived and you are meeting her for the first time. Which of the following actions is MOST appropriate?
    A. Walk up and introduce yourself with a smile and a handshake
    B. Wait for her to come and introduce herself
    C. Approach her and offer a hug to make her feel welcome
    D. Ignore the new hire; she is likely your competition

25. If you are the type of listener who likes to discuss concepts or issues in detail, you would MOST likely fall under which listening style?
    A. Process
    B. Reasons
    C. Results
    D. None of the above

KEY (CORRECT ANSWERS)

1.	A	11.	C
2.	A	12.	C
3.	D	13.	A
4.	A	14.	C
5.	B	15.	B
6.	D	16.	D
7.	C	17.	D
8.	D	18.	B
9.	D	19.	B
10.	B	20.	C

21.	B
22.	D
23.	C
24.	A
25.	A

TEST 2

DIRECTIONS: Each question or incomplete statement is followed by several suggested answers or completions. Select the one that BEST answers the question or completes the statement. *PRINT THE LETTER OF THE CORRECT ANSWER IN THE SPACE AT THE RIGHT.*

1. Which of the following is an example of the BEST practice when communicating in the workplace?
   A. You are horrible with remembering names so you try to use nicknames to cover up for your poor memory.
   B. You only pay attention to the names of people who you work for or who you deem to be "important."
   C. You try to remember everyone's names and use them whenever possible.
   D. None of the above

   1._____

2. Words of civility such as "please" and "thank you" should be used _____ when conversing with coworkers and business partners.
   A. always   B. sometimes   C. rarely   D. never

   2._____

3. When communicating with others, one should _____ stand as close to them as possible and make body contact in order to get an important point across.
   A. always   B. sometimes   C. rarely   D. never

   3._____

4. The MOST appropriate way to end a conversation is to
   A. seek a mutual resolution, but leave abruptly if it continues
   B. find a way to wrap up the conversation so the other person knows it is time to move on
   C. look impatient so hopefully the person will get the hint
   D. tell the other person the conversation should end

   4._____

5. Another name for interpersonal communication in an office setting is
   A. peer-to-peer communication   B. mass communication
   C. virtual reality   D. e-mailing

   5._____

6. Of the following statements, choose the one you feel is the MOST correct.
   A. Devoid of interpersonal communication, people become sick.
   B. Communication is not completely needed for humans.
   C. People are the only animals that need to have relationships in order to survive.
   D. Important communication is not really relevant until after you become an adult.

   6._____

7. John is giving a presentation on ways to communicate effectively with peers. He is having trouble deciding on what to say in his speech.
   Which of the following statements should he AVOID using?
   A. Always try to understand another person's point of view or perspective
   B. Try to imagine what someone is going to say before they actually say it

   7._____

C. Be aware of how non-verbal cues like eye contact and body language affect how your message is received
D. Both B and C

8. Which of the following would MOST affect our perception of communication with coworkers? 8.____
   A. Past experiences B. Marital problems
   C. Rumors spread about coworkers D. None of the above

9. Many people think of communication as both _____ and _____ messages. 9.____
   A. formal; informal B. hearing; listening
   C. sending; receiving D. finding; decoding

10. Why is context important in communication? 10.____
    A. It's important to know which buttons to push in order to get what you want.
    B. Saying something to one person may not have the same effect as saying it to someone else.
    C. Context is only important if you are worried about what others think.
    D. None of the above

11. If your brother is normally bright and talkative during the summer, but you notice he gets quiet and subdued in the winter, the MOST likely communication context he is dealing with would be 11.____
    A. relational   B. cultural   C. inner   D. physical

12. _____ is an example of a negative nonverbal action you can take. 12.____
    A. Smiling
    B. Using a tone of voice that matches your message
    C. Maintaining eye contact
    D. Slumping your shoulders

13. Cultural context can BEST be described as 13.____
    A. what people think of as it relates to the event they are participating in (i.e., wedding versus a funeral)
    B. the connection between a father and his son
    C. rules and patterns of Americans versus the Japanese
    D. thoughts, feelings, and sensations inside a person's head

14. Which of the following BEST describes feedback? 14.____
    A. Staring at the speaker while he talks
    B. Nodding and smiling while listening to a speaker
    C. Standing an appropriate distance away so the speaker does not get uncomfortable
    D. Trying to speak while the other person is speaking because you have something more important to say

15. Being able to communicate more effectively can be improved upon by
    A. continually making an effort to be as flexible as possible when talking to others
    B. committing to one style of speaking until you master it
    C. using the same style of correspondence as the person with whom you are speaking
    D. always using the opposite style of communication from the person you are speaking to

16. John walks up to Sally and compliments her on the dress she wore to work today. In his mind, John was just being friendly, but Sally went to her manager and filed a harassment charge against John.
    This miscommunication could MOST easily be classified as an error in what?
    A. Reality   B. Perception   C. Friendship   D. Loyalty

17. If a speaker's tone is flat and monotone, which of the following is the MOST likely reaction that listeners will have?
    They will
    A. enthused by the message
    B. enjoy the message but not be overly excited about it
    C. be polite and interested but will not seem very engaged
    D. be bored and uninterested in the message

18. When Steve speaks to his group about his ideas, he generally has a higher pitch to his voice and gesticulates frequently.
    This lead his team members to believe that Steve
    A. is enthusiastic and has great ideas for the group
    B. has had too much caffeine and needs to relax
    C. is trying to show off for the boss and make them look bad
    D. is extremely smart and great at his job

19. _____ is used when a person wants to add stress to key words in communication. It lets the audience understand the mood or feelings of particular words or phrases.
    A. Anger   B. Tone   C. Perception   D. Inflection

20. If Barry tells Bill that his haircut looks "great" and Bill can tell Barry is being insincere, which of the following tones is Barry MOST likely using?
    A. Affectionate   B. Apologetic   C. Threatening   D. Sarcastic

21. As a supervisor, it is important that everyone clearly comprehends everything you communicate to them.
    In order to ensure this happens, which of the following things should you avoid?
    A. Overusing jargon
    B. Explaining something more than once
    C. Speaking slowly and annunciating everything
    D. Having meetings in the morning

22. If your supervisor is looking down at the ground or has his back to you as he is speaking, it MOST clearly indicates to those who are listening to him that the supervisor
    A. is shy and doesn't like speaking in front of people
    B. is disinterested and doesn't care what he's talking about
    C. is approachable and friendly
    D. dislikes his job and wants to get out as soon as possible

23. Interpersonal communication helps you
    A. know what others are thinking
    B. turn into an inspiring speaker, especially in public
    C. learn about yourself
    D. communicate with the general public

24. In general, people who smile more are perceived as
    A. devious   B. friendly
    C. attractive   D. easy to manipulate

25. If your supervisor constantly takes advantage of you and expresses his or her opinion often at the expense of you or other workers, which communication style are they MOST likely using?
    A. Nonassertive   B. Assertive   C. Aggressive   D. Peacemaking

---

KEY (CORRECT ANSWERS)

1.	C		11.	D
2.	A		12.	D
3.	D		13.	C
4.	B		14.	B
5.	A		15.	A
6.	A		16.	B
7.	B		17.	D
8.	A		18.	A
9.	C		19.	D
10.	B		20.	D

21. A
22. B
23. D
24. B
25. C

EXAMINATION SECTION
TEST 1

DIRECTIONS: Each question or incomplete statement is followed by several suggested answers or completions. Select the one that BEST answers the question or completes the statement. *PRINT THE LETTER OF THE CORRECT ANSWER IN THE SPACE AT THE RIGHT.*

1. Although some kinds of instructions are best put in written form, a supervisor can give many instructions verbally.
   In which one of the following situations would verbal instructions be MOST suitable?
   A. Furnishing an employee with the details to be checked in doing a certain job
   B. Instructing an employee on the changes necessary to update the office manual used in your unit
   C. Informing a new employee where different kinds of supplies and equipment that he might need are kept
   D. Presenting an assignment to an employee who will be held accountable for following a series of steps

   1._____

2. You may be asked to evaluate the organization structure of your unit.
   Which one of the following questions would you NOT expect to take up in an evaluation of this kind?
   A. Is there an employee whose personal problems are interfering with his or her work?
   B. Is there an up-to-date job description for each position in this section?
   C. Are related operations and tasks grouped together and regularly assigned together?
   D. Are responsibilities divided as far as possible, and is this division clearly understood by all employees?

   2._____

3. In order to distribute and schedule work fairly and efficiently, a supervisor may wish to make a work distribution study. A simple way of getting the information necessary for such a study is to have everyone for one week keep track of each task doe and the time spent on each.
   Which one of the following situations showing up in such study would MOST clearly call for corrective action?
   A. The newest employee takes longer to do most tasks than do experienced employees.
   B. One difficult operation takes longer to do than most other operations carried out by the section.
   C. A particular employee is very frequently assigned tasks that are not similar and have no relationship to each other.
   D. The most highly skilled employee is often assigned the most difficult jobs.

   3._____

4. The authority to carry out a job can be delegated to a subordinate, but the supervisor remains responsible for the work of the section as a whole.
As a supervisor, which of the following rules would be the BEST one for you to follow in view of the above statement?
   A. Avoid assigning important tasks to your subordinates, because you will be blamed if anything goes wrong
   B. Be sure each subordinate understands the specific job he has been assigned, and check at intervals to make sure assignments are done properly
   C. Assign several people to every important job so that responsibility will be spread out as much as possible
   D. Have an experienced subordinate check all work done by other employees so that there will be little chance of anything going wrong

4.____

5. The human tendency to resist change is often reflected in higher rates of turnover, absenteeism, and errors whenever an important change is made in an organization. Although psychologists do not fully understand the reasons why people resist change, they believe that the resistance stems from a threat to the individual's security, that it is a form of fear of the unknown.
In light of this statement, which one of the following approaches would probably be MOST effective in preparing employees for a change in procedure in their unit?
   A. Avoid letting employees know anything about the change until the last possible moment
   B. Sympathize with employees who resent the change and let them know you share their doubts and fears
   C. Promise the employees that if the change turns out to be a poor one, you will allow them to suggest a return to the old system
   D. Make sure that employees know the reasons for the change and are aware of the benefits that are expected from it

5.____

6. Each of the following methods of encouraging employee participation in work planning has been used effectively with different kinds and sizes of employee groups.
Which one of the following methods would be MOST suitable for a group of four technically skilled employees?
   A. Discussions between the supervisor and a representative of the group
   B. A suggestion program with semi-annual awards for outstanding suggestions
   C. A group discussion summoned whenever a major problem remains unsolved for more than a month
   D. Day-to-day exchange of information, opinions, and experience

6.____

7. Of the following, the MOST important reason why a supervisor is given the authority to tell subordinates what work they should do, how they should do it, and when it should be done is that usually
   A. most people will not work unless there is someone with authority standing over them

7.____

B. work is accomplished more effectively if the supervisor plans and coordinates it
C. when division of work is left up to subordinates, there is constant arguing, and very little work is accomplished
D. subordinates are not familiar with the tasks to be performed

8. Fatigue is a factor that affects productivity in all work situations. However, a brief rest period will ordinarily serve to restore a person from fatigue.
According to this statement, which one of the following techniques is MOST likely to reduce the impact of fatigue on overall productivity in a unit?
   A. Scheduling several short breaks throughout the day
   B. Allowing employees to go home early
   C. Extending the lunch period an extra half hour
   D. Rotating job assignments every few weeks

8._____

9. After giving a new task to an employee, it is a good idea for a supervisor to ask specific questions to make sure that the employee grasps the essentials of the task and sees how it can be carried out. Questions which ask the employee what he thinks or how he feels about an important aspect of the task are particularly effective.
Which one of the following questions is NOT the type of question which would be useful in the foregoing situation?
   A. Do you feel there will be any trouble meeting the 4:30 deadline?
   B. How do you feel about the kind of work we do here?
   C. Do you think that combining those two steps will work all right?
   D. Can you think of any additional equipment you may need for this process?

9._____

10. Of the following, the LEAST important reason for having a *continuous* training program is that
    A. employees may forget procedures that they have already learned
    B. employees may develop shortcuts on the job that result in inaccurate work
    C. the job continue to change because of new procedures and equipment
    D. training is one means of measuring effectiveness and productivity on the job

10._____

11. In training a new employee, it is usually advisable to break down the job into meaningful parts and have the new employee master one part before going on to the next.
Of the following, the BEST reason for using this technique is to
    A. let the new employee know the reason for what he is doing and thus encourage him to remain in the unit
    B. make the employee aware of the importance of the work and encourage him to work harder
    C. show the employee that the work is easy so that he will be encouraged to work faster
    D. make it more likely that the employee will experience success and will be encouraged to continue learning the job

11._____

12. You may occasionally find a serious error in the work of one of your subordinates.
    Of the following, the BEST time to discuss such an error with an employee usually is
    A. immediately after the error is found
    B. after about two weeks, since you will also be able to point out some good things that the employee has accomplished
    C. when you have discovered a pattern of errors on the part of this employee so that he will not be able to dispute your criticism
    D. after the error results in a complaint by your own supervisor

13. For very important announcements to the staff, a supervisor should usually use both written and oral communications. For example, when a new procedure is to be introduced, the supervisor can more easily obtain the group's acceptance by giving his subordinates a rough draft of the new procedure and calling a meeting of all his subordinates.
    The LEAST important benefit of this technique is that it will better enable the supervisor to
    A. explain why the change is necessary
    B. make adjustments in the new procedure to meet valid staff objections
    C. assign someone to carry out the new procedure
    D. answer questions about the new procedure

14. Assume that, while you are interviewing an individual to obtain information, the individual pauses in the middle of an answer.
    The BEST of the following actions for you to take at that time is to
    A. correct any inaccuracies in what he has said
    B. remain silent until he continues
    C. explain your position on the matter being discussed
    D. explain that time is short and that he must complete his story quickly

15. When you are interviewing someone to obtain information, the BEST of the following reasons for you to repeat certain of his exact words is to
    A. assure him that appropriate action will be taken
    B. encourage him to switch to another topic of discussion
    C. assure him that you agree with his point of view
    D. encourage him to elaborate on a point he has made

16. Generally, when writing a letter, the use of precise words and concise sentences is
    A. *good*, because less time will be required to write the letter
    B. *bad*, because it is most likely that the reader will think the letter is unimportant and will not respond favorably
    C. *good*, because it is likely that your desired meaning will be conveyed to the reader
    D. *bad*, because your letter will be too brief to provide adequate information

17. In which of the following cases would it be MOST desirable to have two cards for one individual in a single alphabetic file?
    The individual has
    A. a hyphenated surname
    B. two middle names
    C. a first name with an unusual spelling
    D. a compound first name

18. Of the following, it is MOST appropriate to use a form letter when it is necessary to answer many
    A. requests or inquiries from a single individual
    B. follow-up letters from individuals requesting additional information
    C. request or inquiries about a single subject
    D. complaints from individuals that they have been unable to obtain various types of information

19. Assume that you are asked to make up a budget for your section for the coming year, and you are told that the most important function of the budget is its "control function."
    Of the following, "control" in this context implies MOST NEARLY that
    A. you will probably be asked to justify expenditures in any category when it looks as though these expenditures are departing greatly from the amount budgeted
    B. your section will probably not be allowed to spend more than the budgeted amount in any given category, although it is always permissible to spend less
    C. your section will be required to spend the exact amount budgeted in every category
    D. the budget will be filed in the Office of the Comptroller so that when a year is over the actual expenditures can be compared with the amounts in the budget

20. In writing a report, the practice of taking up the LEAST important points *first* and the most important points *last* is a
    A. *good* technique, since the final points made in a report will make the greatest impression on the reader
    B. *good* technique, since the material is presented in a more logical manner and will lead directly to the conclusions
    C. *poor* technique, since the reader's time is wasted by having to review irrelevant information before finishing the report
    D. *poor* technique, since it may cause the reader to lose interest in the report and arrive at incorrect conclusions about the report

21. Typically, when the technique of "supervision by results" is practiced, higher management sets down, either implicitly or explicitly, certain performance standards or goals that the subordinate is expected to meet. So long as these standards are met, management interferes very little.
    The MOST likely result of the use of this technique is that it will

A. lead to ambiguity in terms of goals
B. be successful only to the extent that close direct supervision is practiced
C. make it possible to evaluate both employee and supervisory effectiveness
D. allow for complete dependence on the subordinate's part

22. When making written evaluations and reviews of the performance of subordinates, it is usually ADVISABLE to
    A. avoid informing the employee of the evaluation if it is critical because it may create hard feelings
    B. avoid informing the employee of the evaluation whether critical or favorable because it is tension-producing
    C. to permit the employee to see the evaluation but not to discuss it with him because the supervisor cannot be certain where the discussion might lead
    D. to discuss the evaluation openly with the employee because it helps the employee understand what is expected of him

23. There are a number of well-known and respected human relations principles that successful supervisors have been using for years in building good relationships with their employees.
    Which of the following does NOT illustrate such a principle?
    A. Give clear and complete instructions
    B. Let each person know how he is getting along
    C. Keep an open-door policy
    D. Make all relationships personal ones

24. Assume that it is necessary for you to give an unpleasant assignment to one of your subordinates. You expect this employee to raise some objections to this assignment.
    The MOST appropriate of the following actions for you to take FIRST is to issue the assignment
    A. *orally*, with the further statement that you will not listen to any complaints
    B. *in writing*, to forestall any complaints by the employee
    C. *orally*, permitting the employee to express his feelings
    D. *in writing*, with a note that any comments should be submitted in writing

25. Suppose you have just announced at a staff meeting with your subordinates that a radical reorganization of work will take place next week. Your subordinates at the meeting appear to be excited, tense, and worried.
    Of the following, the BEST action for you to take at that time is to
    A. schedule private conferences with each subordinate to obtain his reaction to the meeting
    B. close the meeting and tell your subordinates to return immediately to their work assignments
    C. give your subordinates some time to ask questions and discuss your announcement
    D. insist that your subordinates do not discuss your announcement among themselves or with other members of the agency

KEY (CORRECT ANSWERS)

1.	C	11.	D
2.	A	12.	A
3.	C	13.	C
4.	B	14.	B
5.	D	15.	D
6.	D	16.	C
7.	B	17.	A
8.	A	18.	C
9.	B	19.	A
10.	D	20.	D

21. C
22. D
23. D
24. C
25. C

TEST 2

DIRECTIONS: Each question or incomplete statement is followed by several suggested answers or completions. Select the one that BEST answers the question or completes the statement. *PRINT THE LETTER OF THE CORRECT ANSWER IN THE SPACE AT THE RIGHT.*

1. Of the following, the BEST way for a supervisor to increase employees' interest in their work is to
   A. allow them to make as many decisions as possible
   B. demonstrate to them that he is as technically competent as they
   C. give each employee a difficult assignment
   D. promptly convey to them instructions from higher management

   1.____

2. The one of the following which is LEAST important in maintaining a high level of productivity on the part of employees is the
   A. provision of optimum physical working conditions for employees
   B. strength of employees' aspirations for promotion
   C. anticipated satisfactions which employees hope to derive from their work
   D. employees' interest in their jobs

   2.____

3. Of the following, the MAJOR advantage of group problem-solving, as compared to individual problem-solving, is that groups will more readily
   A. abide by their own decisions
   B. agree with agency management
   C. devise new policies and procedures
   D. reach conclusions sooner

   3.____

4. The group problem-solving conference is a useful supervisory method for getting people to reach solutions to problems.
   Of the following, the reason that groups usually reach more realistic solutions than do individuals is that
   A. individuals, as a rule, take longer than do groups in reaching decisions and are, therefore, more likely to make an error
   B. bringing people together to let them confer impresses participants with the seriousness of problems
   C. groups are generally more concerned with the future in evaluating organizational problems
   D. the erroneous opinions of group members tend to be corrected by the other members

   4.____

5. A competent supervisor should be able to distinguish between human and technical problems.
   Of the following, the MAJOR difference between such problems is that serious human problems, in comparison to ordinary technical problems
   A. are remedied more quickly
   B. involve a lesser need for diagnosis
   C. are more difficult to define
   D. become known through indications which are usually the actual problem

   5.____

6. Of the following, the BEST justification for a public agency establishing an alcoholism program for its employees is that
   A. alcoholism has traditionally been looked upon with a certain amused tolerance by management and thereby ignored as a serious illness
   B. employees with drinking problems have twice as many on-the-job accidents, especially during the early years of the problem
   C. excessive use of alcohol is associated with personality instability hindering informal social relationships among peers and subordinates
   D. the agency's public reputation will suffer despite an employee's drinking problem being a personal matter of little public concern

7. Assume you are a manager and you find a group of maintenance employees assigned to your project drinking and playing cards for money in an incinerator room after their regular working hours.
   The one of the following actions it would be BEST for you to take is to
   A. suspend all employees immediately if there is no question in your mind as to the validity of the charges
   B. review the personnel records of those involved with the supervisor and make a joint decision on which employees should sustain penalties of loss of annual leave or fines
   C. ask the supervisor to interview each violator and submit written reports to you and thereafter consult with the supervisor about disciplinary actions
   D. deduct three days of annual leave from each employee involved if he pleads guilty in lieu of facing more serious charges

8. Assume that as a manager you must discipline a subordinate, but all of the pertinent facts necessary for a full determination of the appropriate action to take are not yet available. However, you fear that a delay in disciplinary action may damage the morale of other employees.
   The one of the following which is MOST appropriate for you to do in this matter is to
   A. take immediate disciplinary action as if all the pertinent facts were available
   B. wait until all pertinent facts are available before reaching a decision
   C. inform the subordinate that you know he is guilty, issue a stern warning, and then let him wait for your further action
   D. reduce the severity of the discipline appropriate for the violation

9. There are two standard dismissal procedures utilized by most public agencies. The first is the "open back door" policy, in which the decision of a supervisor in discharging an employee for reasons of inefficiency cannot be cancelled by the central personnel agency. The second is the "closed back door" policy, in which the central personnel agency can order the supervisor to restore the discharged employee to his position.
   Of the following, the major DISADVANTAGE of the "closed back door" policy as opposed to the "open back door" policy is that central personnel agencies are
   A. likely to approve the dismissal of employees when there is inadequate justification

B. likely to revoke dismissal actions out of sympathy for employees
C. less qualified than employing agencies to evaluate the efficiency of employees
D. easily influenced by political, religious, and racial factors

10. The one of the following for which a formal grievance-handling system is LEAST useful is in
    A. reducing the frequency of employee complaints
    B. diminishing the likelihood of arbitrary action by supervisors
    C. providing an outlet for employee frustrations
    D. bringing employee problems to the attention of higher management

11. The one of the following managers whose leadership style involves the GREATEST delegation of authority to subordinates is the one who presents to subordinates
    A. his ideas and invites questions
    B. his decision and persuades them to accept it
    C. the problem, gets their suggestions, and makes his decision
    D. a tentative decision which is subject to change

12. Which of the following is MOST likely to cause employee productivity standards to be set too high?
    A. Standards of productivity are set by first-line supervisors rather than by higher level managers.
    B. Employees' opinions about productivity standards are sought through written questionnaires.
    C. Initial studies concerning productivity are conducted by staff specialists.
    D. Ideal work conditions assumed in the productivity standards are lacking in actual operations.

13. The one of the following which states the MAIN value of an organization chart for a manager is that such charts show the
    A. lines of formal authority
    B. manner in which duties are performed by each employee
    C. flow of work among employees on the same level
    D. specific responsibilities of each position

14. Which of the following BEST names the usual role of a line unit with regard to the organization's programs?
    A. Seeking publicity
    B. Developing
    C. Carrying out
    D. Evaluating

15. Critics of promotion *from within* a public agency argue for hiring *from outside* the agency because they believe that promotion from within leads to
    A. resentment and consequent weakened morale on the part of those not promoted
    B. the perpetuation of outdated practices and policies
    C. a more complex hiring procedure than hiring from outside the agency
    D. problems of objectively appraising someone already in the organization

16. The one of the following management functions which usually can be handled MOST effectively by a committee is the
    A. settlement of interdepartmental disputes
    B. planning of routine work schedules
    C. dissemination of information
    D. assignment of personnel

16._____

17. Assume that you are serving on a committee which is considering proposals in order to recommend a new maintenance policy. After eliminating a number of proposals by unanimous consent, the committee is deadlocked on three proposals.
    The one of the following which is the BEST way for the committee to reach agreement on a proposal they could recommend is to
    A. consider and vote on each proposal separately by secret ballot
    B. examine and discuss the three proposals until the proponents of two of them are persuaded they are wrong
    C. reach a synthesis which incorporates the significant features of each proposals
    D. discuss the three proposals until the proponents of each one concede those aspects of the proposals about which there is disagreement

17._____

18. A commonly used training and development method for professional staff is the case method, which utilizes the description of a situation, real or simulated, to provide a common base for analysis, discussion, and problem-solving.
    Of the following, the MOST appropriate time to use the case method is when professional staff needs
    A. insight into their personality problems
    B. practice in applying management concepts to their own problems
    C. practical experience in the assignment of delegated responsibilities
    D. to know how to function in many different capacities

18._____

19. The incident process is a training and development method in which trainees are given a very brief statement of an event or o a situation presenting a job incident or an employee problem of special significance.
    Of the following, it is MOST appropriate to use the incident process when
    A. trainees need to learn to review and analyze facts before solving a problem
    B. there are a large number of trainees who require the same information
    C. there are too many trainees to carry on effective discussion
    D. trainees are not aware of the effect of their behavior on others

19._____

20. The one of the following types of information about which a clerical employee is usually LEAST concerned during the orientation process is
    A. his specific job duties
    B. where he will work
    C. his organization's history
    D. who his associates will be

20._____

21. The one of the following which is the MOST important limitation on the degree to which work should be broken down into specialized tasks is the point at which
    A. there ceases to be sufficient work of a specialized nature to occupy employees
    B. training costs equal the half-yearly savings derived from further specialization
    C. supervision of employees performing specialized tasks becomes more technical than supervision of general employees
    D. it becomes more difficult to replace the specialist than to replace the generalist who performs a complex set of functions

22. When a supervisor is asked for his opinion of the suitability for promotion of a subordinate, the supervisor is actually being asked to predict the subordinate's future behavior in a new role.
    Such a prediction is MOST likely to be accurate if the
    A. higher position is similar to the subordinate's current one
    B. higher position requires intangible personal qualities
    C. new position has had little personal association with the subordinate away from the job

23. In one form of the non-directive evaluation interview, the supervisor communicates his evaluation to the employee and then listens to the employee's response without making further suggestions.
    The one of the following which is the PRINCIPAL danger of this method of evaluation is that the employee is MOST likely to
    A. develop an indifferent attitude towards the supervisor
    B. fail to discover ways of improving his performance
    C. become resistant to change in the organization's structure
    D. place the blame for his shortcomings on his co-workers

24. In establishing rules for his subordinates, a superior should be PRIMARILY concerned with
    A. creating sufficient flexibility to allow for exceptions
    B. making employees aware of the reasons for the rules and the penalties for infractions
    C. establishing the strength of his own position in relation to his subordinates
    D. having his subordinates know that such rules will be imposed in a personal manner

25. The practice of conducting staff training sessions on a periodic basis is generally considered
    A. *poor*; it takes employees away from their work assignments
    B. *poor*; all staff training should be done on an individual basis
    C. *good*; it permits the regular introduction of new methods and techniques
    D. *good*; it ensures a high employee productivity rate

KEY (CORRECT ANSWERS)

1.	A	11.	C
2.	A	12.	D
3.	A	13.	A
4.	D	14.	C
5.	C	15.	B
6.	B	16.	A
7.	C	17.	C
8.	B	18.	B
9.	C	19.	A
10.	A	20.	C

21. A
22. A
23. B
24. B
25. C

EXAMINATION SECTION
TEST 1

DIRECTIONS: Each question or incomplete statement is followed by several suggested answers or completions. Select the one that BEST answers the question or completes the statement. *PRINT THE LETTER OF THE CORRECT ANSWER IN THE SPACE AT THE RIGHT.*

1. Following are three statements concerning on-the-job training: 1.____
   I. On-the-job training is rarely used as a method of training employees.
   II. On-the-job training is often carried on with little or no planning.
   III. On-the-job training is often less expensive than other types.
   Which of the following BEST classifies the above statements into those that are correct and those that are not?
   A. I is correct, but II and III are not.   B. II is correct but I and III are not.
   C. I and II are correct, but III is not.   D. II and III are correct, but I is not.

2. The one of the following which is NOT a valid principle for a supervisor to keep 2.____
   in mind when talking to a subordinate about his performance is:
   A. People frequently know when they deserve criticism.
   B. Supervisors should be prepared to offer suggestions to subordinates about how to improve their work.
   C. Good points should be discussed before bad points.
   D. Magnifying a subordinate's faults will get him to improve faster.

3. In many organizations information travels quickly through the grapevine. 3.____
   Following are three statements concerning the *grapevine*:
   I. Information a subordinate does not want to tell her supervisor may reach the supervisor through the *grapevine*.
   II. A supervisor can often do her job better by knowing the information that travels through the *grapevine*.
   III. A supervisor can depend on the *grapevine* as a way to get accurate information from the employees on his staff.
   Which one of the following CORRECTLY classifies the above statements into those which are generally correct and those which are not?
   A. II is correct, but I and III are not.   B. III is correct, but I and II are not.
   C. I and II are correct, but III is not.   D. I and III are correct, but II is not.

4. Following are three statements concerning supervision: 4.____
   I. A supervisor knows he is doing a good job if his subordinates depend upon him to make every decision.
   II. A supervisor who delegates authority to his subordinates soon finds that his subordinates begin to resent him.
   III. Giving credit for good work is frequently an effective method of getting subordinates to work harder

Which one of the following CORRECTLY classifies the above statements into those that are correct and those that are not?
- A. I and II are correct, but III is not.
- B. II and III are correct, but I is not.
- C. II is correct, but I and III are not.
- D. III is correct, but I and II are not.

5. Of the following, the LEAST appropriate action for a supervisor to take in preparing a disciplinary case against a subordinate is to
   - A. keep careful records of each incident in which the subordinate has been guilty of misconduct or incompetency, even though immediate disciplinary action may not be necessary
   - B. discuss with the employee each incident of misconduct as it occurs so the employee knows where he stands
   - C. accept memoranda from any other employees who may have been witnesses to acts of misconduct
   - D. keep the subordinate's personnel file confidential so that he is unaware of the evidence being gathered against him

6. Praise by a supervisor can be an important element in motivating subordinates. Following are three statements concerning a supervisor's praise of subordinates:
   I. In order to be effective, praise must be lavish and constantly restated.
   II. Praise should be given in a manner which meets the needs of the individual subordinate.
   III. The subordinate whose work is praised should believe that the praise is earned.

   Which of the following CORRECTLY classifies the above statements into those that are correct and those that are not?
   - A. I is correct, but II and III are not.
   - B. II and III are correct, but I is not.
   - C. III is correct, but I and II are not.
   - D. I and II are correct, but III is not.

7. A supervisor feels that he is about to lose his temper while reprimanding a subordinate.
   Of the following, the BEST action for the supervisor to take is to
   - A. postpone the reprimand for a short time until his self-control is assured
   - B. continue the reprimand because a loss of temper by the supervisor will show the subordinate the seriousness of the error he made
   - C. continue the reprimand because failure to do so will show that the supervisor does not have complete self-control
   - D. postpone the reprimand until the subordinate is capable of understanding the reason for the supervisor's loss of temper

8. Following are three statements concerning various ways of giving orders to subordinates:
   I. An implied order or suggestion is usually appropriate for the inexperienced employee.
   II. A polite request is less likely to upset a sensitive subordinate than a direct order.
   III. A direct order is usually appropriate in an emergency situation.

Which of the following CORRECTLY classifies the above statements into those that are correct and those that are not?
- A. I is correct, but II and III are not.
- B. II and III are correct, but I is not.
- C. III is correct, but I and II are not.
- D. I and II are correct, but III is not.

9. The one of the following which is NOT an acceptable reason for taking disciplinary action against a subordinate guilty of serious violations of the rules is that
   - A. the supervisor can *let off steam* against subordinates who break rules frequently
   - B. a subordinate whose work continues to be unsatisfactory may be terminated
   - C. a subordinate may be encouraged to improve his work
   - D. an example is set for other employees

10. At the first meeting with your staff after appointment as a supervisor, you find considerable indifference and some hostility among the participants.
    Of the following, the MOST appropriate way to handle this situation is to
    - A. disregard the attitudes displayed and continue to make your presentation until you have completed it
    - B. discontinue your presentation but continue the meeting and attempt to find out the reasons for their attitudes
    - C. warm up your audience with some good-natured statements and anecdotes and then proceed with your presentation
    - D. discontinue the meeting and set up personal interviews with the staff members to try to find out the reason for their attitude

11. Use a written rather than oral communication to amend any previous written communication.
    Of the following, the BEST justification for this statement is that
    - A. oral changes will be considered more impersonal and thus less important
    - B. oral changes will be forgotten or recalled indifferently
    - C. written communications are clearer and shorter
    - D. written communications are better able to convey feeling tone

12. Assume that a certain supervisor, when writing important communications to his subordinates, often repeats certain points in different words.
    This technique is GENERALLY
    - A. *ineffective*; it tends to confuse rather than help
    - B. *effective*; it tends to improve understanding by the subordinates
    - C. *ineffective*; it unnecessarily increases the length of the communication and may annoy the subordinates
    - D. *effective*; repetition is always an advantage in communications

13. In preparing a letter or a report, a supervisor may wish to persuade the reader of the correctness of some idea or course of action.
    The BEST way to accomplish this is for the supervisor to
    - A. encourage the reader to make a prompt decision
    - B. express each idea in a separate paragraph

C. present the subject matter of the letter in the first paragraph
D. state the potential benefits for the reader

14. Effective communications, a basic necessity for successful supervision is a two-way street. A good supervisor needs to listen to, as well as disseminate, information and he must be able to encourage his subordinates to communicate with him.
Which of the following suggestions will contribute LEAST to improving the *listening power* of a supervisor?
    A. Don't assume anything; don't anticipate, and don't let a subordinate think you know what he is going to say
    B. Don't interrupt; let him have his full say even if it requires a second session that day to get the full story
    C. React quickly to his statements so that he knows you are interested, even if you must draw some conclusions prematurely
    D. Try to understand the real need for his talking to you even if it is quite different from the subject under discussion

15. Of the following, the MOST useful approach for the supervisor to take toward the informal employee communications network known as the *grapevine* is to
    A. remain isolated from it, but not take any active steps to eliminate it
    B. listen to it, but not depend on it for accurate information
    C. use it to disseminate confidential information
    D. eliminate it as diplomatically as possible

16. If a supervisor is asked to estimate the number of employees that he believes he will need in his unit in the coming fiscal year, the supervisor should FIRST attempt to learn the
    A. nature and size of the workload his unit will have during that time
    B. cost of hiring and training new employees
    C. average number of employee absences per year
    D. number of employees needed to indirectly support or assist his unit

17. An important supervisory responsibility is coordinating the operations of the unit. This may include setting work schedules, controlling work quality, establishing interim due dates, etc. In order to handle this task, it has been divided into the following five stages:
    I. <u>Determine the steps</u> or sequence required for the tasks to be performed.
    II. <u>Give the orders</u>, either written or oral, to begin work on the tasks.
    III. <u>Check up</u> by following each task to make sure it is proceeding according to plan.
    IV. <u>Schedule the jobs</u> by setting a time for each task of operation to begin and end.
    V. <u>Control the process</u> by correcting conditions which interfere with the plan.
    The MOST logical sequence in which these planning steps should be performed is:
    A. I, II, III, IV, V   B. II, I, V, III, IV   C. I, IV, II, III, V   D. IV, I, II, III, V

18. Assume that a supervisor calls a meeting with the staff under his supervision in order to discuss several proposals. After some discussion, he realizes that he strongly disagrees with one proposal that four of the staff have rather firmly favored.
At this point, he could BEST handle the situation by saying:
    A. *I have the responsibility for this decision, and I must disagree.*
    B. *I am just reminding you that I have had a great deal more experience in these matters.*
    C. *You have presented some good points, but perhaps we could look at it another way.*
    D. *The only way that this proposal can be disposed of is to defer it for further discussion.*

18.____

19. As far as the social activities and groups of his subordinates are concerned, a supervisor in a large organization can BEST strengthen his tools of leadership by
    A. emphasizing the organization as a whole and forbidding the formation of groups
    B. ignoring the groups as much as possible and dealing with each subordinate as an individual
    C. learning about the status structure of employee groups and their values
    D. avoiding any relationship with groups

19.____

20. If a subordinate asks you, his superior, for advice in planning his career in the department, you should
    A. encourage him to feel that he can easily reach the top of his occupational ladder
    B. discourage him from setting his hopes too high
    C. discuss career opportunities realistically with him
    D. explain that you have no control over his opportunities for advancement

20.____

21. A supervisor's evaluation of an employee is usually based upon a combination of objective facts and subjective judgments or opinions.
Which of the following aspects of an employee's work or performance is MOST likely to be subjectively evaluated?
    A. Quantity   B. Accuracy   C. Attitude   D. Attendance

21.____

22. Of the following possible characteristics of supervisors, the one MOST likely to lead to failure as a supervisor is
    A. a tendency to seek several opinions before making decisions in complex matters
    B. lack of a strong desire to advance to a top position in management
    C. little formal training in human relations skills
    D. poor relations with subordinates and other supervisory personnel

22.____

23. People who break rules do so for a number of reasons. However, employees will break rules LESS often if
    A. the supervisor uses his own judgment about work methods
    B. the supervisor pretends to act strictly, but isn't really serious about it
    C. they greatly enjoy their work
    D. they have completed many years of service

24. Assume that an employee under your supervision has become resentful and generally non-cooperative after his request for transfer to another office closer to his place of residence was denied. The request was denied primarily because of the importance of his current assignment. The employee has been a valued worker, but you are now worried that his resentful attitude will have a detrimental effect.
    Of the following, the MOST desirable way for you to handle this situation is to
    A. arrange for the employee's transfer to the office he originally requested
    B. arrange for the employee's transfer to another office, but not the one he originally requested
    C. attempt to re-focus the employee's attention on those aspects of his current assignment which will be most rewarding and satisfying to him
    D. explain to the employee that, while you are sympathetic to his request, department rules will not allow transfers for reasons of personal convenience

25. Of the following, it would be LEAST advisable for a supervisor to use his administrative authority to affect the behavior and activities of his subordinates when he is trying to
    A. change the way his subordinates perform a particular task
    B. establish a minimum level of conformity to established rules
    C. bring about change in the attitudes of his subordinates
    D. improve the speed with which his subordinates respond to his orders

26. Assume that a supervisor gives his subordinate instructions which are appropriate and clear. The subordinate thereupon refuses to follow these instructions.
    Of the following, it would then be MOST appropriate for the supervisor to
    A. attempt to find out what it is that the employee objects to
    B. take disciplinary action that same day
    C. remind the subordinate about supervisory authority and threaten him with discipline
    D. insist that the subordinate carry out the order immediately

27. Of the following, the MOST effective way to identify training needs resulting from gradual changes in procedure is to
    A. monitor on a continuous basis the actual jobs performed and the skills required
    B. periodically send out a written questionnaire asking personnel to identify their needs
    C. conduct interviews at regular intervals with selected employees
    D. consult employees' personnel records

28. Assume that you, as a supervisor, have had a new employee assigned to you. If the duties of his position can be broken into independent parts, which of the following is usually the BEST way to train this new employee?
Start with
    A. the easiest duties and progressively proceed to the most difficult
    B. something easy; move to something difficult; then back to something easy
    C. something difficult; move to something easy; then to something difficult
    D. the most difficult duties and progressively proceed to the easiest

28._____

29. The oldest and most commonly used training technique is on-the-job training. Instruction is given to the worker by his supervisor or by another employee. Such training is essential in most jobs, although it is not always effective when used alone.
This technique, however, can be effectively used alone if
    A. the skills involved can be learned quickly
    B. a large number of people are to be trained at one time
    C. other forms of training have not been previously used with the people involved
    D. the skills to be taught are mental rather than manual

29._____

30. It is generally agreed that the learning process is facilitated in proportion to the amount of feedback that the learner is given about his performance.
Following are three statements concerning the learning process:
    I. The more specific the learner's knowledge of how he performed, the more rapid his improvement and the higher his level of performance
    II. Giving the learner knowledge of his results does not affect his motivation to learn.
    III. Learners who are not given feedback will set up subjective criteria and evaluate their own performance.
Which of the following choices lists ALL of the above statements that are generally CORRECT?
    A. I and II only   B. I and III only   C. II and III only   D. I, II, and III

30._____

KEY (CORRECT ANSWERS)

1.	D	11.	B	21.	C
2.	D	12.	B	22.	D
3.	C	13.	D	23.	C
4.	D	14.	C	24.	C
5.	D	15.	B	25.	C
6.	B	16.	A	26.	A
7.	A	17.	C	27.	A
8.	B	18.	C	28.	A
9.	A	19.	C	29.	A
10.	D	20.	C	30.	B

TEST 2

DIRECTIONS: Each question or incomplete statement is followed by several suggested answers or completions. Select the one that BEST answers the question or completes the statement. *PRINT THE LETTER OF THE CORRECT ANSWER IN THE SPACE AT THE RIGHT.*

Questions 1-6.

DIRECTIONS: Questions 1 through 6 are to be answered SOLELY on the basis of the information given in the following paragraph.

    The use of role-playing as a training technique was developed during the past decade by social scientists, particularly psychologists, who have been active in training experiments. Originally, this technique was applied by clinical psychologists who discovered that a patient appears to gain understanding of an emotionally disturbing situation when encouraged to act out roles in that situation. As applied in government and business organizations, the purpose of role-playing is to aid employees to understand certain work problems involving interpersonal relations and to enable observers to evaluate various reactions to them. Thus, for example, on the problem of handling grievances, two individuals from the group might be selected to act out extemporaneously the parts of subordinate and supervisor. When this situation is enacted by various pairs among the class and the techniques and results are discussed, the members of the group are presumed to reach conclusions about the most effective means of handling similar situations. Often the use of role reversal, where participants take parts different from their actual work roles, assists individuals to gain more insight into other people's problems and viewpoints. Although role-playing can be a rewarding training device, the trainer must be aware of his responsibilities. If this technique is to be successful, thorough briefing of both actors and observers as to the situation in question, the participants' roles, and what to look for, is essential.

1. The role-playing technique was FIRST used for the purpose of   1.____
   A. measuring the effectiveness of training programs
   B. training supervisors in business organizations
   C. treating emotionally disturbed patients
   D. handling employee grievances

2. When role-playing is used in private business as a training device, the CHIEF aim is to   2.____
   A. develop better relations between supervisor and subordinate in the handling of grievances
   B. come up with a solution to a specific problem that has arisen
   C. determine the training needs of the group
   D. increase employee understanding of the human relation factors in work situations

3. From the above passage, it is MOST reasonable to conclude that when role-playing is used, it is preferable to have the roles acted out by   3.____
   A. only one set of actors   B. no more than 2 sets of actors
   C. several different sets of actors   D. the trainer or trainers of the group

4. Based on the above passage, a trainer using the technique of role reversal in a problem of first-line supervision should assign a senior employee to play the part of a(n)
    A. new employee
    B. senior employee
    C. principal employee
    D. angry citizen

5. It can be inferred from the above passage that a limitation of role-play as a training method is that
    A. many work situations do not lend themselves to role-play
    B. employees are not experienced enough as actors to play the roles realistically
    C. only trainers who have psychological training can use it successfully
    D. participants who are observing and not acting do not benefit from it

6. To obtain good results from the use of role-playing in training, a trainer should give participants
    A. a minimum of information about the situation so that they can act spontaneously
    B. scripts which illustrate the best method for handling the situation
    C. a complete explanation of the problem and the roles to be acted out
    D. a summary of work problems which involve interpersonal relations

7. Of the following, the MOST important reason for a supervisor to prepare good written reports is that
    A. a supervisor is rated on the quality of his reports
    B. decisions are often made on the basis of the reports
    C. such reports take less time for superiors to review
    D. such reports demonstrate efficiency of department operations

8. Of the following, the BEST test of a good report is whether it
    A. provides the information needed
    B. shows the good sense of the writer
    C. is prepared according to a proper format
    D. is grammatical and neat

9. When a supervisor writes a report, he can BEST show that he has an understanding of the subject of the report by
    A. including necessary facts and omitting non-essential details
    B. using statistical data
    C. giving his conclusions but not the data on which they are based
    D. using a technical vocabulary

10. Suppose you and another supervisor on the same level are assigned to work together on a report. You disagree strongly with one of the recommendations the other supervisor wants to include in the report but you cannot change his views.
    Of the following, it would be BEST that
    A. you refuse to accept responsibility for the report
    B. you ask that someone else be assigned to this project to replace you

C. each of you state his own ideas about this recommendation in the report
D. you give in to the other supervisor's opinion for the sake of harmony

11. Standardized forms are often provided for submitting reports.
Of the following, the MOST important advantage of using standardized forms for reports is that
   A. they take less time to prepare than individually written reports
   B. necessary information is less likely to be omitted
   C. the responsibility for preparing these reports can be delegated to subordinates
   D. the person making the report can omit information he considers unimportant

12. A report which may BEST be classed as a *periodic* report is one which
   A. requires the same type of information at regular intervals
   B. contains detailed information which is to be retained in permanent records
   C. is prepared whenever a special situation occurs
   D. lists information in graphic form

13. Which one of the following is NOT an important reason for keeping accurate records in an office?
   A. Facts will be on hand when decisions have to be made.
   B. The basis for past actions can be determined.
   C. Information needed by other bureaus can be furnished.
   D. Filing is easier when records are properly made out.

14. Suppose you are preparing to write a report recommending a change in a certain procedure. You learn that another supervisor made a report a few years ago suggesting a change in this same procedure, but that no action was taken.
Of the following, it would be MOST desirable for you to
   A. avoid reading the other supervisor's report so that you will write with a more up-to-date point of view
   B. make no recommendation since management seems to be against any change in the procedure
   C. read the other report before you write your report to see what bearing it may have on your recommendations
   D. avoid including in your report any information that can be obtained by referring to the other report

15. If a report you are preparing to your superior is going to be a very long one, it would be DESIRABLE to include a summary of your basic conclusions
   A. at the end of the report
   B. at the beginning of the report
   C. in a separate memorandum
   D. right after you present the supporting data

16. Suppose that some bureau and department policies must be very frequently applied by your subordinates while others rarely come into use.
As a supervising employee, a GOOD technique for you to use in fulfilling your responsibility of seeing to it that policies are adhered to is to
    A. ask the director of the bureau to issue to all employees an explanation in writing of all policies
    B. review with your subordinates every week those policies which have daily application
    C. follow up on and explain at regular intervals the application of those policies which are not used very often by your subordinates
    D. recommend to your superiors that policies rarely used be changed or dropped

17. The BASIC purpose behind the principle of delegation of authority is to
    A. give the supervisor who is delegating a chance to acquire skills in higher level functions
    B. free the supervisor from routine tasks in order that he may do the important parts of his job
    C. prevent supervisors from overstepping the lines of authority which have been established
    D. place the work delegated in the hands of those employees who can perform it best

18. A district commander can BEST assist management in long-range planning by
    A. reporting to his superiors any changing conditions in the district
    B. maintaining a neat and efficiently run office
    C. scheduling work so that areas with a high rate of non-compliance get more intensive coverage
    D. properly training new personnel assigned to his district

19. Suppose that new quarters have been rented for your district office.
Of the following, the LEAST important factor to be considered in planning the layout of the office is the
    A. need for screening confidential activities from unauthorized persons
    B. relative importance of the various types of work
    C. areas of noise concentration
    D. convenience with which communication between sections of the office can be achieved

20. Of the following, the MOST basic effect of organizing a department so that lines of authority are clearly defined and duties are specifically assigned is to
    A. increase the need for close supervision
    B. decreases the initiative of subordinates
    C. lessen the possibility of duplication of work
    D. increase the responsibilities of supervisory personnel

21. An accepted management principle is that decisions should be delegated to the lowest point in the organization at which they can be made effectively.
The one of the following which is MOST likely to be a result of the application of this principle is that
    A. no factors will be overlooked in making decisions
    B. prompt action will follow the making of decisions
    C. decisions will be made more rapidly
    D. coordination of decisions that are made will be simplified

22. Suppose you are a supervisor and need some guidance from a higher authority. In which one of the following situations would it be PERMISSIBLE for you to bypass the regular upward channels of communication in the chain of command?
    A. In an emergency when your superior is not available
    B. When it is not essential to get a quick reply
    C. When you feel your immediate superior is not understanding of the situation
    D. When you want to obtain information that you think your superior does not have

23. Of the following, the CHIEF limitation of the organization chart as it is generally used in business and government is that the chart
    A. makes lines of responsibility and authority undesirably definite and formal
    B. is often out of date as soon as it is completed
    C. does not show human factors and informal working relationships
    D. is usually too complicated

24. The *span of control* for any supervisor is the
    A. number of tasks he is expected to perform himself
    B. amount of office space he and his subordinates occupy
    C. amount of work he is responsible for getting out
    D. number of subordinates he can supervise effectively

25. Of the following duties performed by a supervising employee, which would be considered a LINE function rather than a staff function?
    A. Evaluation of office personnel
    B. Recommendations for disciplinary action
    C. Initiating budget requests for replacement of equipment
    D. Inspections, at irregular times, of conditions and staff in the field

KEY (CORRECT ANSWERS)

1. C
2. D
3. C
4. A
5. A

6. C
7. B
8. A
9. A
10. C

11. B
12. A
13. D
14. C
15. B

16. C
17. B
18. A
19. B
20. C

21. B
22. A
23. C
24. D
25. D

READING COMPREHENSION
UNDERSTANDING AND INTERPRETING WRITTEN MATERIAL
EXAMINATION SECTION
TEST 1

Questions 1-8.

DIRECTIONS: Each question or incomplete statement is followed by several suggested answers or completions. Select the one that BEST answers the question or completes the statement. *PRINT THE LETTER OF THE CORRECT ANSWER IN THE SPACE AT THE RIGHT.*

Questions 1 and 2.

DIRECTIONS: Your answers to Questions 1 and 2 must be based ONLY on the information given in the following paragraph.

Hospitals maintained wholly by public taxation may treat only those compensation cases which are emergencies and may not treat such emergency cases longer than the emergency exists; provided, however, that these restrictions shall not be applicable where there is not available a hospital other than a hospital maintained wholly by taxation.

1. According to the above paragraph, compensation cases

    A. are regarded as emergency cases by hospitals maintained wholly by public taxation
    B. are seldom treated by hospitals maintained wholly by public taxation
    C. are treated mainly by privately endowed hospitals
    D. may be treated by hospitals maintained wholly by public taxation if they are emergencies

2. According to the above paragraph, it is MOST reasonable to conclude that where a privately endowed hospital is available,

    A. a hospital supported wholly by public taxation may treat emergency compensation cases only so long as the emergency exists
    B. a hospital supported wholly by public taxation may treat any compensation cases
    C. a hospital supported wholly by public taxation must refer emergency compensation cases to such a hospital
    D. the restrictions regarding the treatment of compensation cases by a tax-supported hospital are not wholly applicable

Questions 3-7.

DIRECTIONS: Answer Questions 3 through 7 ONLY according to the information given in the following passage.

THE MANUFACTURE OF LAUNDRY SOAP

The manufacture of soap is not a complicated process. Soap is a fat or an oil, plus an alkali, water and salt. The alkali used in making commercial laundry soap is caustic soda. The salt used is the same as common table salt. A fat is generally an animal product that is not a liquid at room temperature. If heated, it becomes a liquid. An oil is generally liquid at room temperature. If the temperature is lowered, the oil becomes a solid just like ordinary fat.

At the soap plant, a huge tank five stories high, called a *kettle,* is first filled part way with fats and then the alkali and water are added. These ingredients are then heated and boiled together. Salt is then poured into the top of the boiling solution; and as the salt slowly sinks down through the mixture, it takes with it the glycerine which comes from the melted fats. The product which finally comes from the kettle is a clear soap which has a moisture content of about 34%. This clear soap is then chilled so that more moisture is driven out. As a result, the manufacturer finally ends up with a commercial laundry soap consisting of 88% clear soap and only 12% moisture.

3. An ingredient used in making laundry soap is

   A. table sugar
   B. potash
   C. glycerine
   D. caustic soda

4. According to the above passage, a difference between fats and oils is that fats

   A. cost more than oils
   B. are solid at room temperature
   C. have less water than oils
   D. are a liquid animal product

5. According to the above passage, the MAIN reason for using salt in the manufacture of soap is to

   A. make the ingredients boil together
   B. keep the fats in the kettle melted
   C. remove the glycerine
   D. prevent the loss of water from the soap

6. According to the passage, the purpose of chilling the clear soap is to

   A. stop the glycerine from melting
   B. separate the alkali from the fats
   C. make the oil become solid
   D. get rid of more moisture

7. According to the passage, the percentage of moisture in commercial laundry soap is

   A. 12%   B. 34%   C. 66%   D. 88%

8. The x-ray has gone into business. Developed primarily to aid in diagnosing human ills, the machine now works in packing plants, in foundries, in service stations, and in a dozen ways to contribute to precision and accuracy in industry.
   The above statement means *most nearly* that the x-ray

   A. was first developed to aid business
   B. is of more help to business than it is to medicine
   C. is being used to improve the functioning of business
   D. is more accurate for packing plants than it is for foundries

8.____

Questions 9-25.

DIRECTIONS: Each question consists of a statement. You are to indicate whether the statement is TRUE (T) or FALSE (F). *PRINT THE LETTER OF THE CORRECT ANSWER IN THE SPACE AT THE RIGHT.*

Questions 9-12.

DIRECTIONS: Read the paragraph below about *shock* and then answer Questions 9 through 12 according to the information given in the paragraph.

SHOCK

While not found in all injuries, shock is present in all serious injuries caused by accidents. During shock, the normal activities of the body slow down. This partly explains why one of the signs of shock is a pale, cold skin, since insufficient blood goes to the body parts during shock.

9. If the injury caused by an accident is serious, shock is sure to be present.   9.____

10. In shock, the heart beats faster than normal.   10.____

11. The face of a person suffering from shock is usually red and flushed.   11.____

12. Not enough blood goes to different parts of the body during shock.   12.____

Questions 13-18.

DIRECTIONS: Questions 13 through 18, inclusive, are to be answered SOLELY on the basis of the information contained in the following statement and NOT upon any other information you may have.

Blood transfusions are given to patients at the hospital upon recommendation of the physicians attending such cases. The physician fills out a *Request for Blood Transfusion* form in duplicate and sends both copies to the Medical Director's office, where a list is maintained of persons called *donors* who desire to sell their blood for transfusions. A suitable donor is selected, and the transfusion is given. Donors are, in many instances, medical students and employees of the hospital. Donors receive twenty-five dollars for each transfusion.

13. According to the above paragraph, a blood donor is paid twenty-five dollars for each transfusion.   13.____

14. According to the above paragraph, only medical students and employees of the hospital are selected as blood donors. 14.___

15. According to the above paragraph, the *Request for Blood Transfusion* form is filled out by the patient and sent to the Medical Director's office. 15.___

16. According to the above paragraph, a list of blood donors is maintained in the Medical Director's office. 16.___

17. According to the above paragraph, cases for which the attending physicians recommend blood transfusions are usually emergency cases. 17.___

18. According to the above paragraph, one copy of the *Request for Blood Transfusion* form is kept by the patient and one copy is sent to the Medical Director's office. 18.___

Questions 19-25.

DIRECTIONS: Questions 19 through 25, inclusive, are to be answered SOLELY on the basis of the information contained in the following passage and NOT upon any other information you may have.

Before being admitted to a hospital ward, a patient is first interviewed by the Admitting Clerk, who records the patient's name, age, sex, race, birthplace, and mother's maiden name. This clerk takes all of the money and valuables that the patient has on his person. A list of the valuables is written on the back of the envelope in which the valuables are afterwards placed. Cash is counted and placed in a separate envelope, and the amount of money and the name of the patient are written on the outside of the envelope. Both envelopes are sealed, fastened together, and placed in a compartment of a safe.

An orderly then escorts the patient to a dressing room where the patient's clothes are removed and placed in a bundle. A tag bearing the patient's name is fastened to the bundle. A list of the contents of the bundle is written on property slips, which are made out in triplicate. The information contained on the outside of the envelopes containing the cash and valuables belonging to the patient is also copied on the property slips.

According to the above passage,

19. patients are escorted to the dressing room by the Admitting Clerk. 19.___

20. the patient's cash and valuables are placed together in one envelope. 20.___

21. the number of identical property slips that are made out when a patient is being admitted to a hospital ward is three. 21.___

22. the full names of both parents of a patient are recorded by the Admitting Clerk before a patient is admitted to a hospital ward. 22.___

23. the amount of money that a patient has on his person when admitted to the hospital is entered on the patient's property slips. 23.___

24. an orderly takes all the money and valuables that a patient has on his person. 24.___

25. the patient's name is placed on the tag that is attached to the bundle containing the patient's clothing. 25.___

KEY (CORRECT ANSWERS)

1.	D	11.	F
2.	A	12.	T
3.	D	13.	T
4.	B	14.	F
5.	C	15.	F
6.	D	16.	T
7.	A	17.	T
8.	C	18.	F
9.	T	19.	F
10.	F	20.	F
21.	T		
22.	F		
23.	T		
24.	F		
25.	T		

TEST 2

DIRECTIONS: Each question or incomplete statement is followed by several suggested answers or completions. Select the one that BEST answers the question or completes the statement. *PRINT THE LETTER OF THE CORRECT ANSWER IN THE SPACE AT THE RIGHT.*

Questions 1-4.

DIRECTIONS: Questions 1 through 4 are to be answered in accordance with the following paragraphs.

One fundamental difference between the United States health care system and the health care systems of some European countries is the way that hospital charges for long-term illnesses affect their citizens.

In European countries such as England, Sweden, and Germany, citizens can face, without fear, hospital charges due to prolonged illness, no matter how substantial they may be. Citizens of these nations are required to pay nothing when they are hospitalized, for they have prepaid their treatment as taxpayers when they were well and were earning incomes.

On the other hand, the United States citizen, in spite of the growth of payments by third parties which include private insurance carriers as well as public resources, has still to shoulder 40 percent of hospital care costs, while his private insurance contributes only 25 percent and public resources the remaining 35 percent.

Despite expansion of private health insurance and social legislation in the United States, out-of-pocket payments for hospital care by individuals have steadily increased. Such payments, currently totalling $23 billion, are nearly twice as high as ten years ago.

Reform is inevitable and, when it comes, will have to reconcile sharply conflicting interests. Hospital staffs are demanding higher and higher wages. Hospitals are under pressure by citizens, who as patients demand more and better services but who as taxpayers or as subscribers to hospital insurance plans, are reluctant to pay the higher cost of improved care. An acceptable reconciliation of these interests has so far eluded legislators and health administrators in the United States.

1. According to the above passage, the one of the following which is an ADVANTAGE that citizens of England, Sweden, and Germany have over United States citizens is that, when faced with long-term illness,

    A. the amount of out-of-pocket payments made by these European citizens is small when compared to out-of-pocket payments made by United States citizens
    B. European citizens have no fear of hospital costs no matter how great they may be
    C. more efficient and reliable hospitals are available to the European citizen than is available to the United States citizens
    D. a greater range of specialized hospital care is available to the European citizens than is available to the United States citizens

1.___

2. According to the above passage, reform of the United States system of health care must reconcile all of the following EXCEPT

   A. attempts by health administrators to provide improved hospital care
   B. taxpayers' reluctance to pay for the cost of more and better hospital services
   C. demands by hospital personnel for higher wages
   D. insurance subscribers' reluctance to pay the higher costs of improved hospital care

3. According to the above passage, the out-of-pocket payments for hospital care that individuals made ten years ago was APPROXIMATELY _____ billion.

   A. $32   B. $23   C. $12   D. $3

4. According to the above passage, the GREATEST share of the costs of hospital care in the United States is paid by

   A. United States citizens
   B. private insurance carriers
   C. public resources
   D. third parties

Questions 5-8.

DIRECTIONS: Questions 5 through 8 are to be answered SOLELY on the basis of the information contained in the following passage.

Effective cost controls have been difficult to establish in most hospitals in the United States. Ways must be found to operate hospitals with reasonable efficiency without sacrificing quality and in a manner that will reduce the amount of personal income now being spent on health care and the enormous drain on national resources. We must adopt a new public objective of providing higher quality health care at significantly lower cost. One step that can be taken to achieve this goal is to carefully control capital expenditures for hospital construction and expansion. Perhaps the way to start is to declare a moratorium on all hospital construction and to determine the factors that should be considered in deciding whether a hospital should be built. Such factors might include population growth, distance to the nearest hospital, availability of medical personnel, and hospital bed shortage.

A second step to achieve the new objective is to increase the ratio of out-of-hospital patient to in-hospital patient care. This can be done by using separate health care facilities other than hospitals to attract patients who have increasingly been going to hospital clinics and overcrowding them. Patients should instead identify with a separate health care facility to keep them out of hospitals.

A third step is to require better hospital operating rules and controls. This step might include the review of a doctor's performance by other doctors, outside professional evaluations of medical practice, and required refresher courses and re-examinations for doctors. Other measures might include obtaining mandatory second opinions on the need for surgery in order to avoid unnecessary surgery, and outside review of work rules and procedures to eliminate unnecessary testing of patients.

A fourth step is to halt the construction and public subsidizing of new medical schools and to fill whatever needs exist in professional coverage by emphasizing the medical training of physicians with specialities that are in short supply and by providing a better geographic distribution of physicians and surgeons.

5. According to the above passage, providing higher quality health care at lower cost can be achieved by the

   A. greater use of out-of-hospital facilities
   B. application of more effective cost controls on doctors' fees
   C. expansion of improved in-hospital patient care services at hospital clinics
   D. development of more effective training programs in hospital administration

6. According to the above passage, the one of the following which should be taken into account in determining if a hospital should be constructed is the

   A. number of out-of-hospital health care facilities
   B. availability of public funds to subsidize construction
   C. number of hospitals under construction
   D. availability of medical personnel

7. According to the above passage, it is IMPORTANT to operate hospitals efficiently because

   A. they are currently in serious financial difficulties
   B. of the need to reduce the amount of personal income going to health care
   C. the quality of health care services has deteriorated
   D. of the need to increase productivity goals to take care of the growing population in the United States

8. According to the above passage, which one of the following approaches is MOST LIKELY to result in better operating rules and controls in hospitals?

   A. Allocating doctors to health care facilities on the basis of patient population
   B. Equalizing the workloads of doctors
   C. Establishing a physician review board to evaluate the performance of other physicians
   D. Eliminating unnecessary outside review of patient testing

Questions 9-14.

DIRECTIONS: Questions 9 through 14 are to be answered SOLELY on the basis of the information contained in the following passage.

The United States today is the only major industrial nation in the world without a system of national health insurance or a national health service. Instead, we have placed our prime reliance on private enterprise and private health insurance to meet the need. Yet, in a recent year, of the 180 million Americans under 65 years of age, 34 million had no hospital insurance, 38 million had no surgical insurance, 63 million had no out-patient x-ray and laboratory insurance, 94 million had no insurance for prescription drugs, and 103 million had no insurance for physician office visits or home visits. Some 35 million Americans under the age of 65 had no health insurance whatsoever. Some 64 million additional Americans under age 65 had health insurance coverage that was less than that provided to the aged under Medicare.

Despite more than three decades of enormous growth, the private health insurance industry today pays benefits equal to only one-third of the total cost of private health care, leaving the rest to be borne by the patient—essentially the same ratio which held true a decade ago. Moreover, nearly all private health insurance is limited; it provides partial benefits, not comprehensive benefits; acute care, not preventive care; it siphons off the young and healthy, and ignores the poor and medically indigent. The typical private carrier usually pays only the cost of hospital care, forcing physicians and patients alike to resort to wasteful and inefficient use of hospital facilities, thereby giving further impetus to the already soaring costs of hospital care. Valuable hospital beds are used for routine tests and examinations. Unnecessary hospitalization, unnecessary surgery, and unnecessarily extended hospital stays are encouraged. These problems are exacerbated by the fact that administrative costs of commercial carriers are substantially higher than they are for Blue Shield, Blue Cross, or Medicare.

9. According to the above passage, the PROPORTION of total private health care costs paid by private health insurance companies today as compared to ten years ago has

    A. *increased* by approximately one-third
    B. *remained* practically the same
    C. *increased* by approximately two-thirds
    D. *decreased* by approximately one-third

10. According to the above passage, the one of the following which has contributed MOST to wasteful use of hospital facilities is the

    A. increased emphasis on preventive health care
    B. practice of private carriers of providing comprehensive health care benefits
    C. increased hospitalization of the elderly and the poor
    D. practice of a number of private carriers of paying only for hospital care costs

11. Based on the information in the above passage, which one of the following patients would be LEAST likely to receive benefits from a typical private health insurance plan?
    A

    A. young patient who must undergo an emergency appendectomy
    B. middle-aged patient who needs a costly series of x-ray and laboratory tests for diagnosis of gastrointestinal complaints
    C. young patient who must visit his physician weekly for treatment of a chronic skin disease
    D. middle-aged patient who requires extensive cancer surgery

12. Which one of the following is the MOST accurate inference that can be drawn from the above passage?

    A. Private health insurance has failed to fully meet the health care needs of Americans.
    B. Most Americans under age 65 have health insurance coverage better than that provided to the elderly under Medicare.
    C. Countries with a national health service are likely to provide poorer health care for their citizens than do countries that rely primarily on private health insurance.
    D. Hospital facilities in the United States are inadequate to meet the nation's health care needs.

13. Of the total number of Americans under age 65, what percentage belonged in the combined category of persons with NO health insurance or health insurance less than that provided to the aged under Medicare?

    A. 19%   B. 36%   C. 55%   D. 65%

14. According to the above passage, the one of the following types of health insurance which covered the SMALLEST number of Americans under age 65 was

    A. hospital insurance
    B. surgical insurance
    C. insurance for prescription drugs
    D. insurance for physician office or home visits

Questions 15-17.

DIRECTIONS: Questions 15 through 17 are to be answered SOLELY on the basis of the information contained in the following passage.

Statistical studies have demonstrated that disease and mortality rates are higher among the poor than among the more affluent members of our society. Periodic surveys conducted by the United States Public Health Service continue to document a higher prevalence of infectious and chronic diseases within low income families. While the basic life style and living conditions of the poor are to a considerable extent responsible for this less favorable health status, there are indications that the kind of health care received by the poor also plays a significant role. The poor are less likely to be aware of the concepts and practices of scientific medicine and less likely to seek health care when they need it. Moreover, they are discouraged from seeking adequate health care by the depersonalization, disorganization, and inadequate emphasis on preventive care which characterize the health care most often provided for them.

To achieve the objective of better health care for the poor, the following approaches have been suggested: encouraging the poor to seek preventive care as well as care for acute illness and to establish a lasting one-to-one relationship with a single physician who can treat the poor patient as a whole individual; sufficient financial subsidy to put the poor on an equal footing with *paying patients,* thereby giving them the opportunity to choose from among available health services providers; inducements to health services providers to establish public clinics in poverty areas; and legislation to provide for health education, earlier detection of disease, and coordinated health care.

15. According to the above passage, the one of the following which is a function of the United States Public Health Service is

    A. gathering data on the incidence of infectious diseases
    B. operating public health clinics in poverty areas lacking private physicians
    C. recommending legislation for the improvement of health care in the United States
    D. encouraging the poor to participate in programs aimed at the prevention of illness

16. According to the above passage, the one of the following which is MOST characteristic of the health care currently provided for the poor is that it

   A. aims at establishing clinics in poverty areas
   B. enables the poor to select the health care they want through the use of financial subsidies
   C. places insufficient stress on preventive health care
   D. over-emphasizes the establishment of a one-to-one relationship between physician and patient

17. The above passage IMPLIES that the poor lack the financial resources to

   A. obtain adequate health insurance coverage
   B. select from among existing health services
   C. participate in health education programs
   D. lobby for legislation aimed at improving their health care

Questions 18-20.

DIRECTIONS: Questions 18 through 20 are to be answered SOLELY on the basis of the information contained in the following passage.

The concept of *affiliation,* developed more than ten years ago, grew out of a series of studies which found evidence of faulty care, surgery of *questionable* value and other undesirable conditions in the city's municipal hospitals. The affiliation agreements signed shortly thereafter were designed to correct these deficiencies by assuring high quality medical care. In general, the agreements provided the staff and expertise of a voluntary hospital—sometimes connected with a medical school—to operate various services or, in some cases, all of the professional divisions of a specific municipal hospital. The municipal hospitals have paid for these services, which last year cost the city $200 million, the largest single expenditure of the Health and Hospitals Corporation. In addition, the municipal hospitals have provided to the voluntary hospitals such facilities as free space for laboratories and research. While some experts agree that affiliation has resulted in improvements in some hospital care, they contend that many conditions that affiliation was meant to correct still exist. In addition, accountability procedures between the Corporation and voluntary hospitals are said to be so inadequate that audits of affiliation contracts of the past five years revealed that there may be more than $200 million in charges for services by the voluntary hospitals which have not been fully substantiated. Consequently, the Corporation has proposed that future agreements provide accountability in terms of funds, services supplied, and use of facilities by the voluntary hospitals.

18. According to the above passage, *affiliation* may BEST be defined as an agreement whereby

   A. voluntary hospitals pay for the use of municipal hospital facilities
   B. voluntary and municipal hospitals work to eliminate duplication of services
   C. municipal hospitals pay voluntary hospitals for services performed
   D. voluntary and municipal hospitals transfer patients to take advantage of specialized services

19. According to the above passage, the MAIN purpose for setting up the *affiliation* agreement was to

    A. supplement the revenues of municipal hospitals
    B. improve the quality of medical care in municipal hospitals
    C. reduce operating costs in municipal hospitals
    D. increase the amount of space available to municipal hospitals

20. According to the above passage, inadequate accountability procedures have resulted in

    A. unsubstantiated charges for services by the voluntary hospitals
    B. emphasis on research rather than on patient care in municipal hospitals
    C. unsubstantiated charges for services by the municipal hospitals
    D. economic losses to voluntary hospitals

Questions 21-25.

DIRECTIONS: Questions 21 through 25 are to be answered SOLELY on the basis of the information contained in the following passage.

The payment for medical services covered under the Outpatient Medical Insurance Plan (OMI) may be made, by OMI, directly to a physician or to the OMI patient. If the physician and the patient agree that the physician is to receive payment directly from OMI, the payment will be officially assigned to the physician; this is the assignment method. If payment is not assigned, the patient receives payment directly from OMI based on an itemized bill he submits, regardless of whether or not he has already paid his physician.

When a physician accepts assignment of the payment for medical services, he agrees that total charges will not be more than the allowed charge determined by the OMI carrier administering the program. In such cases, the OMI patient pays any unmet part of the $85 annual deductible, plus 10 percent of the remaining charges to the physician. In unassigned claims, the patient is responsible for the total amount charged by the physician. The patient will then be reimbursed by the program 90 percent of the allowed charges in excess of the annual deductible.

The rates of acceptance of assignments provide a measure of how many OMI patients are spared *administrative participation* in the program. Because physicians are free to accept or reject assignments, the rate in which assignments are made provide a general indication of the medical community's satisfaction with the OMI program, especially with the level of amounts paid by the program for specific services and the promptness of payment.

21. According to the above passage, in order for a physician to receive payment directly from OMI for medical services to an OMI patient, the physician would have to accept the assignment of payment, to have the consent of the patient, AND to

    A. submit to OMI a paid itemized bill
    B. collect from the patient 90% of the total bill
    C. collect from the patient the total amount of the charges for his services, a portion of which he will later reimburse the patient
    D. agree that his charges for services to the patient will not exceed the amount allowed by the program

22. According to the above passage, if a physician accepts assignment of payment, the patient pays 22.____

    A. the total amount charged by the physician and is reimbursed by the program for 90 percent of the allowed charges in excess of the applicable deductible
    B. any unmet part of the $85 annual deductible, plus 90 percent of the remaining charges
    C. the total amount charged by the physician and is reimbursed by the program for 10 percent of the allowed charges in excess of the $85 annual deductible
    D. any unmet part of the $85 annual deductible, plus 10 percent of the remaining charges

23. A physician has accepted the assignment of payment for charges to an OMI patient. The physician's charges, all of which are allowed under OMI, amount to $115. This is the first time the patient has been eligible for OMI benefits and the first time the patient has received services from this physician. 23.____
    According to the above passage, the patient must pay the physician

    A. $27 B. $76.50 C. $88 D. $103.50

24. In an unassigned claim, a physician's charges, all of which are allowed under OMI, amount to $165. The patient paid the physician the full amount of the bill. 24.____
    If this is the FIRST time the patient has been eligible for OMI benefits, he will receive from OMI a reimbursement of

    A. $72 B. $80 C. $85 D. $93

25. According to the above passage, if the rate of acceptance of assignments by physicians is high, it is LEAST appropriate to conclude that the medical community is generally satisfied with the 25.____

    A. supplementary medical insurance program
    B. levels of amounts paid to physicians by the program
    C. number of OMI patients being spared administrative participation in the program
    D. promptness of the program in making payment for services

KEY (CORRECT ANSWERS)

1. B	11. C	21. D
2. A	12. A	22. D
3. C	13. C	23. C
4. D	14. D	24. A
5. A	15. A	25. C
6. D	16. C	
7. B	17. B	
8. C	18. C	
9. B	19. B	
10. D	20. A	

PREPARING WRITTEN MATERIALS
EXAMINATION SECTION
TEST 1

DIRECTIONS: Each question consists of a sentence which may be classified appropriately under one of the following four categories:
- A. Incorrect because of faulty grammar or sentence structure.
- B. Incorrect because of faulty punctuation.
- C. Incorrect because of faulty spelling or capitalization.
- D. Correct

Examine each sentence carefully. Then, in the space at the right, print the capital letter preceding the option which is the BEST of the four suggested above. All incorrect sentences contain only one type of error. Consider a sentence correct if it contains none of the types of errors mentioned, although there may be other correct ways of expressing the same thought.

1. The fire apparently started in the storeroom, which is usually locked.   1._____

2. On approaching the victim two bruises were noticed by this officer.   2._____

3. The officer, who was there examined the report with great care.   3._____

4. Each employee in the office had a separate desk.   4._____

5. The suggested procedure is similar to the one now in use.   5._____

6. No one was more pleased with the new procedure than the chauffeur.   6._____

7. He tried to pursuade her to change the procedure.   7._____

8. The total of the expenses charged to petty cash were high.   8._____

9. An understanding between him and I was finally reached.   9._____

10. It was at the supervisor's request that the clerk agreed to postpone his vacation.   10._____

11. We do not believe that it is necessary for both he and the clerk to attend the conference.   11._____

12. All employees, who display perseverance, will be given adequate recognition.   12._____

13. He regrets that some of us employees are dissatisfied with our new assignments.   13._____

14. "Do you think that the raise was merited," asked the supervisor? 14._____

15. The new manual of procedure is a valuable supplament to our rules and regulation. 15._____

16. The typist admitted that she had attempted to pursuade the other employees to assist her in her work. 16._____

17. The supervisor asked that all amendments to the regulations be handled by you and I. 17._____

18. They told both he and I that the prisoner had escaped. 18._____

19. Any superior officer, who, disregards the just complaints of his subordinates, is remiss in the performance of his duty. 19._____

20. Only those members of the national organization who resided in the Middle west attended the conference in Chicago. 20._____

21. We told him to give the investigation assignment to whoever was available. 21._____

22. Please do not disappoint and embarass us by not appearing in court. 22._____

23. Despite the efforts of the Supervising mechanic, the elevator could not be started. 23._____

24. The U.S. Weather Bureau, weather record for the accident date was checked. 24._____

KEY (CORRECT ANSWERS)

1.	D	11.	A
2.	A	12.	B
3.	B	13.	D
4.	D	14.	B
5.	D	15.	C
6.	D	16.	C
7.	C	17.	A
8.	A	18.	A
9.	A	19.	B
10.	D	20.	C

21. D
22. C
23. C
24. B

TEST 2

DIRECTIONS: Each question consists of a sentence. Some of the sentences contain errors in English grammar or usage, punctuation, spelling, or capitalization. A sentence does not contain an error simply because it could be written in a different manner. Choose answer:
- A. If the sentence contains an error in English grammar or usage.
- B. if the sentence contains an error in punctuation.
- C. If the sentence contains an error in spelling or capitalization
- D. If the sentence does not contain any errors.

1. The severity of the sentence prescribed by contemporary statutes—including both the former and the revised New York Penal Laws—do not depend on what crime was intended by the offender.   1.____

2. It is generally recognized that two defects in the early law of attempt played a part in the birth of burglary: (1) immunity from prosecution for conduct short of the last act before completion of the crime, and (2) the relatively minor penalty imposed for an attempt (it being a common law misdemeanor) vis-à-vis the completed offense.   2.____

3. The first sentence of the statute is applicable to employees who enter their place of employment, invited guests, and all other persons who have an express or implied license or privilege to enter the premises.   3.____

4. Contemporary criminal codes in the United States generally divide burglary into various degrees, differentiating the categories according to place, time and other attendent circumstances.   4.____

5. The assignment was completed in record time but the payroll for it has not yet been prepaid.   5.____

6. The operator, on the other hand, is willing to learn me how to use the mimeograph.   6.____

7. She is the prettiest of the three sisters.   7.____

8. She doesn't know; if the mail has arrived.   8.____

9. The doorknob of the office door is broke.   9.____

10. Although the department's supply of scratch pads and stationery have diminished considerably, the allotment for our division has not been reduced.   10.____

11. You have not told us whom you wish to designate as your secretary.   11.____

12. Upon reading the minutes of the last meeting, the new proposal was taken up for consideration.   12.____

13. Before beginning the discussion, we locked the door as a precautionery measure. 13._____

14. The supervisor remarked, "Only those clerks, who perform routine work, are permitted to take a rest period." 14._____

15. Not only will this duplicating machine make accurate copies, but it will also produce a quantity of work equal to fifteen transcribing typists. 15._____

16. "Mr. Jones," said the supervisor, "we regret our inability to grant you an extention of your leave of absence." 16._____

17. Although the employees find the work monotonous and fatigueing, they rarely complain. 17._____

18. We completed the tabulation of the receipts on time despite the fact that Miss Smith our fastest operator was absent for over a week. 18._____

19. The reaction of the employees who attended the meeting, as well as the reaction of those who did not attend, indicates clearly that the schedule is satisfactory to everyone concerned. 19._____

20. Of the two employees, the one in our office is the most efficient. 20._____

21. No one can apply or even understand, the new rules and regulations. 21._____

22. A large amount of supplies were stored in the empty office. 22._____

23. If an employee is occassionally asked to work overtime, he should do so willingly. 23._____

24. It is true that the new procedures are difficult to use but, we are certain that you will learn them quickly. 24._____

25. The office manager said that he did not know who would be given a large allotment under the new plan. 25._____

KEY (CORRECT ANSWERS)

1.	A		11.	D
2.	D		12.	A
3.	D		13.	C
4.	C		14.	B
5.	C		15.	A
6.	A		16.	C
7.	D		17.	C
8.	B		18.	B
9.	A		19.	D
10.	A		20.	A

21. B
22. A
23. C
24. B
25. D

TEST 3

DIRECTIONS: Each of the following sentences may be classified MOST appropriately under one of the following categories:
  A. Faulty because of incorrect grammar
  B. Faulty because of incorrect punctuation
  C. Faulty because of incorrect capitalization
  D. Correct

Examine each sentence carefully. Then, in the space at the right, print the capital letter preceding the option which is the BEST of the four suggested above. All incorrect sentence contain but one type of error. Consider a sentence correct if it contains none of the types of errors mentioned, even though there may be other correct ways of expressing the same thought.

1. The desk, as well as the chairs, were moved out of the office.   1._____

2. The clerk whose production was greatest for the month won a day's vacation as first prize.   2._____

3. Upon entering the room, the employees were found hard at work at their desks.   3._____

4. John Smith our new employee always arrives at work on time.   4._____

5. Punish whoever is guilty of stealing the money.   5._____

6. Intelligent and persistent effort lead to success no matter what the job may be.   6._____

7. The secretary asked, "can you call again at three o'clock?"   7._____

8. He told us, that if the report was not accepted at the next meeting, it would have to be rewritten.   8._____

9. He would not have sent the letter if he had known that it would cause so much excitement.   9._____

10. We all looked forward to him coming to visit us.   10._____

11. If you find that you are unable to complete the assignment please notify me as soon as possible.   11._____

12. Every girl in the office went home on time but me; there was still some work for me to finish.   12._____

13. He wanted to know who the letter was addressed to, Mr. Brown or Mr. Smith.   13._____

14. "Mr. Jones, he said, please answer this letter as soon as possible."   14._____

15. The new clerk had an unusual accent inasmuch as he was born and educated in the south. 15._____

16. Although he is younger than her, he earns a higher salary. 16._____

17. Neither of the two administrators are going to attend the conference being held in Washington, D.C. 17._____

18. Since Miss Smith and Miss Jones have more experience than us, they have been given more responsible duties. 18._____

19. Mr. Shaw the supervisor of the stock room maintains an inventory of stationery and office supplies. 19._____

20. Inasmuch as this matter affects both you and I, we should take joint action. 20._____

21. Who do you think will be able to perform this highly technical work? 21._____

22. Of the two employees, John is considered the most competent. 22._____

23. He is not coming home on tuesday; we expect him next week. 23._____

24. Stenographers, as well as typists must be able to type rapidly and accurately. 24._____

25. Having been placed in the safe we were sure that the money would not be stolen. 25._____

KEY (CORRECT ANSWERS)

1.	A	11.	B
2.	D	12.	D
3.	A	13.	A
4.	B	14.	B
5.	D	15.	C
6.	A	16.	A
7.	C	17.	A
8.	B	18.	A
9.	D	19.	B
10.	A	20.	A

21. D
22. A
23. C
24. B
25. A

TEST 4

DIRECTIONS: Each of the following sentences consist of four sentences lettered A, B, C, and D. One of the sentences in each group contains an error in grammar or punctuation. Indicate the INCORRECT sentence in each group. *PRINT THE LETTER OF THE CORRECT ANSWER IN THE SPACE AT THE RIGHT.*

1. A. Give the message to whoever is on duty.
   B. The teacher who's pupil won first prize presented the award.
   C. Between you and me, I don't expect the program to succeed.
   D. His running to catch the bus caused the accident.

   1.____

2. A. The process, which was patented only last year is already obsolete.
   B. His interest in science (which continues to the present) led him to convert his basement into a laboratory.
   C. He described the book as "verbose, repetitious, and bombastic".
   D. Our new director will need to possess three qualities: vision, patience, and fortitude.

   2.____

3. A. The length of ladder trucks varies considerably.
   B. The probationary fireman reported to the officer to who he was assigned.
   C. The lecturer emphasized the need for we firemen to be punctual.
   D. Neither the officers nor the members of the company knew about the new procedure.

   3.____

4. A. Ham and eggs is the specialty of the house.
   B. He is one of the students who are on probation.
   C. Do you think that either one of us have a chance to be nominated for president of the class?
   D. I assume that either he was to be in charge or you were.

   4.____

5. A. Its a long road that has no turn.
   B. To run is more tiring than to walk.
   C. We have been assigned three new reports: namely, the statistical summary, the narrative summary, and the budgetary summary.
   D. Had the first payment been made in January, the second would be due in April.

   5.____

6. A. Each employer has his own responsibilities.
   B. If a person speaks correctly, they make a good impression.
   C. Every one of the operators has had her vacation.
   D. Has anybody filed his report?

   6.____

7. A. The manager, with all his salesmen, was obliged to go.
   B. Who besides them is to sign the agreement?
   C. One report without the others is incomplete.
   D. Several clerks, as well as the proprietor, was injured.

   7.____

106

2 (#4)

8. A. A suspension of these activities is expected.
    B. The machine is economical because first cost and upkeep are low.
    C. A knowledge of stenography and filing are required for this position.
    D. The condition in which the goods were received shows that the packing was not done properly.

8.____

9. A. There seems to be a great many reasons for disagreement.
    B. It does not seem possible that they could have failed.
    C. Have there always been too few applicants for these positions?
    D. There is no excuse for these errors.

9.____

10. A. We shall be pleased to answer your question.
    B. Shall we plan the meeting for Saturday?
    C. I will call you promptly at seven.
    D. Can I borrow your book after you have read it?

10.____

11. A. You are as capable as I.
    B. Everyone is willing to sign but him and me.
    C. As for he and his assistant, I cannot praise them too highly.
    D. Between you and me, I think he will be dismissed.

11.____

12. A. Our competitors bid above us last week.
    B. The survey which was began last year has not yet been completed.
    C. The operators had shown that they understood their instructions.
    D. We have never ridden over worse roads.

12.____

13. A. Who did they say was responsible?
    B. Whom did you suspect?
    C. Who do you suppose it was?
    D. Whom do you mean?

13.____

14. A. Of the two propositions, this is the worse.
    B. Which report do you consider the best—the one in January or the one in July?
    C. I believe this is the most practicable of the many plans submitted.
    D. He is the youngest employee in the organization.

14.____

15. A. The firm had but three orders last week.
    B. That doesn't really seem possible.
    C. After twenty years scarcely none of the old business remains.
    D. Has he done nothing about it?

15.____

KEY (CORRECT ANSWERS)

1. B
2. A
3. C
4. C
5. A
6. B
7. D
8. C
9. A
10. D
11. C
12. B
13. A
14. B
15. C

PREPARING WRITTEN MATERIAL
EXAMINATION SECTION
TEST 1

DIRECTIONS: Each question or incomplete statement is followed by several suggested answers or completions. Select the one that BEST answers the question or completes the statement. *PRINT THE LETTER OF THE CORRECT ANSWER IN THE SPACE AT THE RIGHT.*

1. The one of the following sentences which is LEAST acceptable from the viewpoint of correct usage is:
    A. The police thought the fugitive to be him.
    B. The criminals set a trap for whoever would fall into it.
    C. It is ten years ago since the fugitive fled from the city.
    D. The lecturer argued that criminals are usually cowards.
    E. The police removed four bucketfuls of earth from the scene of the crime.

1.____

2. The one of the following sentences which is LEAST acceptable from the viewpoint of correct usage is:
    A. The patrolman scrutinized the report with great care.
    B. Approaching the victim of the assault, two bruises were noticed by the patrolman.
    C. As soon as I had broken down the door, I stepped into the room.
    D. I observed the accused loitering near the building, which was closed at the time.
    E. The storekeeper complained that his neighbor was guilty of violating a local ordinance.

2.____

3. The one of the following sentences which is LEAST acceptable from the viewpoint of correct usage is:
    A. I realized immediately that he intended to assault the woman, so I disarmed him.
    B. It was apparent that Mr. Smith's explanation contained many inconsistencies.
    C. Despite the slippery condition of the street, he managed to stop the vehicle before injuring the child.
    D. Not a single one of them wish, despite the damage to property, to make a formal complaint.
    E. The body was found lying on the floor.

3.____

4. The one of the following sentences which contains NO error in usage is:
    A. After the robbers left, the proprietor stood tied in his chair for about two hours before help arrived.
    B. In the cellar I found the watchman's hat and coat.
    C. The persons living in adjacent apartments stated that they had heard no unusual noises.

4.____

D. Neither a knife or any firearms were found in the room.
E. Walking down the street, the shouting of the crowd indicated that something was wrong.

5. The one of the following sentences which contains NO error in usage is:
   A. The policeman lay a firm hand on the suspect's shoulder.
   B. It is true that neither strength nor agility are the most important requirement for a good patrolman.
   C. Good citizens constantly strive to do more than merely comply the restraints imposed by society.
   D. No decision was made as to whom the prize should be awarded.
   E. Twenty years is considered a severe sentence for a felony.

5._____

6. Which of the following sentences is NOT expressed in standard English usage?
   A. The victim reached a pay-phone booth and manages to call police headquarters.
   B. By the time the call was received, the assailant had left the scene.
   C. The victim has been a respected member of the community for the past eleven years.
   D. Although the lighting was bad and the shadows were deep, the storekeeper caught sight of the attacker.
   E. Additional street lights have since been installed, and the patrols have been strengthened.

5._____

7. Which of the following sentences is NOT expressed in standard English usage?
   A. The judge upheld the attorney's right to question the witness about the missing glove.
   B. To be absolutely fair to all parties is the jury's chief responsibility.
   C. Having finished the report, a loud noise in the next room startled the sergeant.
   D. The witness obviously enjoyed having played a part in the proceedings.
   E. The sergeant planned to assign the case to whoever arrived first.

7._____

8. In which of the following sentences is a word misused?
   A. As a matter of principle, the captain insisted that the suspect's partner be brought for questioning.
   B. The principle suspect had been detained at the station house for most of the day.
   C. The principal in the crime had no previous criminal record, but his closest associate had been convicted of felonies on two occasions.
   D. The interest payments had been made promptly, but the firm had been drawing upon the principal for these payments.
   E. The accused insisted that his high school principal would furnish him a character reference.

8._____

9. Which of the following statements is ambiguous?
   A. Mr. Sullivan explained why Mr. Johnson had been dismissed from his job.
   B. The storekeeper told the patrolman he had made a mistake.
   C. After waiting three hours, the patients in the doctor's office were sent home.
   D. The janitor's duties were to maintain the building in good shape and to answer tenants' complaints.
   E. The speed limit should, in my opinion, be raised to sixty miles an hour on that stretch of road.

10. In which of the following is the punctuation or capitalization faulty?
    A. The accident occurred at an intersection in the Kew Gardens section of Queens, near the bus stop.
    B. The sedan, not the convertible, was struck in the side.
    C. Before any of the patrolmen had left the police car received an important message from headquarters.
    D. The dog that had been stolen was returned to his master, John Dempsey, who lived in East Village.
    E. The letter had been sent to 12 Hillside Terrace, Rutland, Vermont 05702.

Questions 11-25.

DIRECTIONS: Questions 11 through 25 are to be answered in accordance with correct English usage; that is, standard English rather than nonstandard or substandard. Nonstandard and substandard English includes words or expressions usually classified as slang, dialect, illiterate, etc., which are not generally accepted as correct in current written communication. Standard English also requires clarity, proper punctuation and capitalization and appropriate use of words. Write the letter of the sentence NOT expressed in standard English usage in the space at the right.

11. A. There were three witnesses to the accident.
    B. At least three witnesses were found to testify for the plaintiff.
    C. Three of the witnesses who took the stand was uncertain about the defendant's competence to drive.
    D. Only three witnesses came forward to testify for the plaintiff.
    E. The three witnesses to the accident were pedestrians.

12. A. The driver had obviously drunk too many martinis before leaving for home.
    B. The boy who drowned had swum in these same waters many times before.
    C. The petty thief had stolen a bicycle from a private driveway before he was apprehended.
    D. The detectives had brung in the heroin shipment they intercepted.
    E. The passengers had never ridden in a converted bus before.

13. A. Between you and me, the new platoon plan sounds like a good idea.
    B. Money from an aunt's estate was left to his wife and he.
    C. He and I were assigned to the same patrol for the first time in two months.
    D. Either you or he should check the front door of that store.
    E. The captain himself was not sure of the witness's reliability.

14. A. The alarm had scarcely begun to ring when the explosion occurred.
    B. Before the firemen arrived at the scene, the second story had been destroyed.
    C. Because of the dense smoke and heat, the firemen could hardly approach the now-blazing structure.
    D. According to the patrolman's report, there wasn't nobody in the store when the explosion occurred.
    E. The sergeant's suggestion was not at all unsound, but no one agreed with him.

15. A. The driver and the passenger they were both found to be intoxicated.
    B. The driver and the passenger talked slowly and not too clearly.
    C. Neither the driver nor his passengers were able to give a coherent account of the accident.
    D. In a corner of the room sat the passenger, quietly dozing.
    E. the driver finally told a strange and unbelievable story, which the passenger contradicted.

16. A. Under the circumstances I decided not to continue my examination of the premises.
    B. There are many difficulties now not comparable with those existing in 1960.
    C. Friends of the accused were heard to announce that the witness had better been away on the day of the trial.
    D. The two criminals escaped in the confusion that followed the explosion.
    E. The aged man was struck by the considerateness of the patrolman's offer.

17. A. An assemblage of miscellaneous weapons lay on the table.
    B. Ample opportunities were given to the defendant to obtain counsel.
    C. The speaker often alluded to his past experience with youthful offenders in the armed forces.
    D. The sudden appearance of the truck aroused my suspicions.
    E. Her studying had a good affect on her grades in high school.

18. A. He sat down in the theater and began to watch the movie.
    B. The girl had ridden horses since she was four years old.
    C. Application was made on behalf of the prosecutor to cite the witness for contempt.
    D. The bank robber, with his two accomplices, were caught in the act.
    E. His story is simply not credible.

19. A. The angry boy said that he did not like those kind of friends.
     B. The merchant's financial condition was so precarious that he felt he must avail himself of any offer of assistance.
     C. He is apt to promise more than he can perform.
     D. Looking at the messy kitchen, the housewife felt like crying.
     E. A clerk was left in charge of the stolen property.

20. A. His wounds were aggravated by prolonged exposure to sub-freezing temperatures.
     B. The prosecutor remarked that the witness was not averse to changing his story each time he was interviewed.
     C. The crime pattern indicated that the burglars were adapt in the handling of explosives.
     D. His rigid adherence to a fixed plan brought him into renewed conflict with his subordinates.
     E. He had anticipated that the sentence would be delivered by noon.

21. A. The whole arraignment procedure is badly in need of revision.
     B. After his glasses were broken in the fight, he would of gone to the optometrist if he could.
     C. Neither Tom nor Jack brought his lunch to work.
     D. He stood aside until the quarrel was over.
     E. A statement in the psychiatrist's report disclosed that the probationer vowed to have his revenge.

22. A. His fiery and intemperate speech to the striking employees fatally affected any chance of a future reconciliation.
     B. The wording of the statute has been variously construed.
     C. The defendant's attorney, speaking in the courtroom, called the official a demagogue who contempuously disregarded the judge's orders.
     D. The baseball game is likely to be the most exciting one this year.
     E. The mother divided the cookies among her two children.

23. A. There was only a bed and a dresser in the dingy room.
     B. John was one of the few students that have protested the new rule.
     C. It cannot be argued that the child's testimony is negligible; it is, on the contrary, of the greatest importance.
     D. The basic criterion for clearance was so general that officials resolved any doubts in favor of dismissal.
     E. Having just returned from a long vacation, the officer found the city unbearably hot.

24. A. The librarian ought to give more help to small children.
     B. The small boy was criticized by the teacher because he often wrote careless.
     C. It was generally doubted whether the women would permit the use of her apartment for intelligence operations.
     D. The probationer acts differently every time the officer visits him.
     E. Each of the newly appointed officers has 12 years of service.

25.
A. The North is the most industrialized region in the country.
B. L. Patrick Gray 3d, the bureau's acting director, stated that, while "rehabilitation is fine" for some convicted criminals, "it is a useless gesture for those who resist every such effort."
C. Careless driving, faulty mechanism, narrow or badly kept roads all play their part in causing accidents.
D. The childrens' books were left in the bus.
E. It was a matter of internal security; consequently, he felt no inclination to rescind his previous order.

25.____

KEY (CORRECT ANSWERS)

1.	C	11.	C
2.	B	12.	D
3.	D	13.	B
4.	C	14.	D
5.	E	15.	A
6.	A	16.	C
7.	C	17.	E
8.	B	18.	D
9.	B	19.	A
10.	C	20.	C

21. B
22. E
23. B
24. B
25. D

TEST 2

DIRECTIONS: Each question or incomplete statement is followed by several suggested answers or completions. Select the one that BEST answers the question or completes the statement. *PRINT THE LETTER OF THE CORRECT ANSWER IN THE SPACE AT THE RIGHT.*

Questions 1-6.

DIRECTIONS: Each of Questions 1 through 6 consists of a statement which contains a word (one of those underlined) that is either incorrectly used because it is not in keeping with the meaning the quotation is evidently intended to convey, or is misspelled. There is only one INCORRECT word in each quotation. Of the four underlined words, determine if the first one should be replaced by the word lettered A, the second replaced by the word lettered B, the third replaced by the word lettered C, or the fourth replaced by the word lettered D.

1. Whether one depends on fluorescent or artificial light or both, adequate standards should be maintained by means of systematic tests. 1.____
   A. natural   B. safeguards   C. established   D. routine

2. A police officer has to be prepared to assume his knowledge as a social scientist in the community. 2.____
   A. forced   B. role   C. philosopher   D. street

3. It is practically impossible to indicate whether a sentence is too long simply by measuring its length. 3.____
   A. almost   B. tell   C. very   D. guessing

4. Strong leaders are required to organize a community for delinquency prevention and for dissemination of organized crime and drug addiction. 4.____
   A. tactics   B. important   C. control   D. meetings

5. The demonstrators who were taken to the Criminal Courts building in Manhattan (because it was large enough to accommodate them), contended that the arrests were unwarranted. 5.____
   A. demonstraters   B. Manhatten
   C. accomodate   D. unwarranted

6. They were guaranteed a calm atmosphere, free from harassment, which would be conducive to quiet consideration of the indictments. 6.____
   A. guarenteed   B. atmspher
   C. harassment   D. inditements

Questions 7-11.

DIRECTIONS: Each of Questions 7 through 11 consists of a statement containing four words in capital letters. One of these words in capital letters is not in keeping with the meaning which the statement is evidently intended to carry. The four words in capital letters in each statement are reprinted after the statement. Print the capital letter preceding the one of the four words which does MOST to spoil the true meaning of the statement in the space at the right.

7. Retirement and pension systems are essential not only to provide employees with with a means of support in the future, but also to prevent longevity and CHARITABLE considerations from UPSETTING the PROMOTIONAL opportunities RETIRED members of the career service.
   A. charitable   B. upsetting   C. promotional   D. retired

7.____

8. Within each major DIVISION in a properly set up public or private organization, provision is made so that each NECESSARY activity is CARED for and lines of authority and responsibility are clear-cut and INFINITE.
   A. division   B. necessary   C. cared   D. infinite

8.____

9. In public service, the scale of salaries paid must be INCIDENTAL to the services rendered, with due CONSIDERATION for the attraction of the desired MANPOWER and for the maintenance of a standard of living COMMENSURATE with the work to be performed.
   A. incidental   B. consideration
   C. manpower   D. commensurate

9.____

10. An understanding of the AIMS of an organization by the staff will AID greatly in increasing the DEMAND of the correspondence work of the office, and will to a large extent DETERMINE the nature of the correspondence.
    A. aims   B. aid   C. demand   D. determine

10.____

11. BECAUSE the Civil Service Commission strongly feels that the MERIT system is a key factor in the MAINTENANCE of democratic government, it has adopted as one of its major DEFENSES the progressive democratization of its own procedures in dealing with candidates for positions in the public service.
    A. Because   B. merit   C. maintenance   D. defenses

11.____

Questions 12-14.

DIRECTIONS: Questions 12 through 14 consist of one sentence each. Each sentence contains an incorrectly used word. First, decide which is the incorrectly used word. Then, from among the options given, decide which word, when substituted for the incorrectly used word, makes the meaning of the sentence clear.
EXAMPLE:
The U.S. national income exhibits a pattern of long term deflection.
   A. reflection   B. subjection   C. rejoicing   D. growth

The word *deflection* in the sentence does not convey the meaning the sentence evidently intended to convey. The word *growth* (Answer D), when substituted for the word *deflection*, makes the meaning of the sentence clear. Accordingly, the answer to the question is D.

12. The study commissioned by the joint committee fell compassionately short of the mark and would have to be redone.
    A. successfully
    B. insignificantly
    C. experimentally
    D. woefully

13. He will not idly exploit any violation of the provisions of the order.
    A. tolerate
    B. refuse
    C. construe
    D. guard

14. The defendant refused to be virile and bitterly protested service.
    A. irked
    B. feasible
    C. docile
    D. credible

Questions 15-25.

DIRECTIONS: Questions 15 through 25 consist of short paragraphs. Each paragraph contains one word which is INCORRECTLY used because it is NOT in keeping with the meaning of the paragraph. Find the word in each paragraph which is INCORRECTLY used and then select as the answer the suggested word which should be substituted for the incorrectly used word.

SAMPLE QUESTION:
In determining who is to do the work in your unit, you will have to decide just who does what from day to day. One of your lowest responsibilities is to assign work so that everybody gets a fair share and that everyone can do his part well.
   A. new   B. old   C. important   D. performance

EXPLANATION:
The word which is NOT in keeping with the meaning of the paragraph is *lowest*. This is the INCORRECTLY used word. The suggested word *important* would be in keeping with the meaning of the paragraph and should be substituted for *lowest*. Therefore, the CORRECT answer is choice C.

15. If really good practice in the elimination of preventable injuries is to be achieved and held in any establishment, top management must refuse full and definite responsibility and must apply a good share of its attention to the task.
    A. accept
    B. avoidable
    C. duties
    D. problem

16. Recording the human face for identification is by no means the only service performed by the camera in the field of investigation. When the trial of any issue takes place, a word picture is sought to be distorted to the court of incidents, occurrences, or events which are in dispute.
    A. appeals
    B. description
    C. portrayed
    D. deranged

17. In the collection of physical evidence, it cannot be emphasized too strongly that a haphazard systematic search at the scene of the crime is vital. Nothing must be overlooked. Often the only leads in a case will come from the results of this search.
    A. important B. investigation C. proof D. thorough

18. If an investigator has reason to suspect that the witness is mentally stable, or a habitual drunkard, he should leave no stone unturned in his investigation to determine if the witness was under the influence of liquor or drugs, or was mentally unbalanced either at the time of the occurrence to which he testified or at the time of the trial.
    A. accused B. clue C. deranged D. question

19. The use of records is a valuable step in crime investigation and is the main reason every department should maintain accurate reports. Crimes are not committed through the use of departmental records alone but from the use of all records, of almost every type, wherever they may be found and whenever they give any incidental information regarding the criminal.
    A. accidental B. necessary C. reported D. solved

20. In the years since passage of the Harrison Narcotic Act of 1914, making the possession of opium amphetamines illegal in most circumstances, drug use has become a subject of considerable scientific interest and investigation. There is at present a voluminous literature on drug use of various kinds.
    A. ingestion B. derivatives C. addiction D. opiates

21. Of course, the fact that criminal laws are extremely patterned in definition does not mean that the majority of persons who violate them are dealt with as criminals. Quite the contrary, for a great many forbidden acts are voluntarily engaged in within situations of privacy and go unobserved and unreported.
    A. symbolic B. casual C. scientific D. broad-gauged

22. The most punitive way to study punishment is to focus attention on the pattern of punitive action: to study how a penalty is applied, too study what is done to or taken from an offender.
    A. characteristic B. degrading C. objective D. distinguished

23. The most common forms of punishment in times past have been death, physical torture, mutilation, branding, public humiliation, fines, forfeits of property, banishment, transportation, and imprisonment. Although this list is by no means differentiated, practically every form of punishment has had several variations and applications.
    A. specific B. simple C. exhaustive D. characteristic

24. There is another important line of inference between ordinary and professional criminals, and that is the source from which they are recruited. The professional criminal seems to be drawn from legitimate employment and, in many instances, from parallel vocations or pursuits. 24.____
    A. demarcation   B. justification   C. superiority   D. reference

25. He took the position that the success of the program was insidious on getting additional revenue. 25.____
    A. reputed   B. contingent   C. failure   D. indeterminate

KEY (CORRECT ANSWERS)

1.	A	11.	D
2.	B	12.	D
3.	B	13.	A
4.	C	14.	C
5.	D	15.	A
6.	C	16.	C
7.	D	17.	D
8.	D	18.	C
9.	A	19.	D
10.	C	20.	B

21.	D
22.	C
23.	C
24.	A
25.	B

TEST 3

DIRECTIONS: Each question or incomplete statement is followed by several suggested answers or completions. Select the one that BEST answers the question or completes the statement. *PRINT THE LETTER OF THE CORRECT ANSWER IN THE SPACE AT THE RIGHT.*

Questions 1-5.

DIRECTIONS: Questions 1 through 5 are to be answered on the basis of the following.

You are a supervising officer in an investigative unit. Earlier in the day, you directed Detectives Tom Dixon and Sal Mayo to investigate a reported assault and robbery in a liquor store within your area of jurisdiction.

Detective Dixon has submitted to you a preliminary investigative report containing the following information:

- At 1630 hours on 2/20, arrived at Joe's Liquor Store at 350 SW Avenue with Detective Mayo to investigate A & R.
- At store interviewed Rob Ladd, store manager, who stated that he and Joe Brown (store owner) had been stuck up about ten minutes prior to our arrival.
- Ladd described the robbers as male whites in their late teens or early twenties. Further stated that one of the robbers displayed what appeared to be an automatic pistol as he entered the store, and said, *Give us the money or we'll kill you.* Ladd stated that Brown then reached under the counter where he kept a loaded .38 caliber pistol. Several shots followed, and Ladd threw himself to the floor.
- The robbers fled, and Ladd didn't know if any money had been taken.
- At this point, Ladd realized that Brown was unconscious on the floor and bleeding from a head wound.
- Ambulance called by Ladd, and Brown was removed by same to General Hospital.
- Personally interviewed John White, 382 Dartmouth Place, who stated he was inside store at the time of occurrence. White states that he hid behind a wine display upon hearing someone say, *Give us the money.* He then heard shots and saw two young men run from the store to a yellow car parked at the curb. White was unable to further describe auto. States the taller of the two men drove the car away while the other sat on passenger side in front.
- Recovered three spent .38 caliber bullets from premises and delivered them to Crime Lab.
- To General Hospital at 1800 hours but unable to interview Brown, who was under sedation and suffering from shock and a laceration of the head.
- Alarm #12487 transmitted for car and occupants.
- Case Active.

Based solely on the contents of the preliminary investigation submitted by Detective Dixon, select one sentence from the following groups of sentences which is MOST accurate and is grammatically correct.

1. A. Both robbers were armed.
   B. Each of the robbers were described as a male white.
   C. Neither robber was armed.
   D. Mr. Ladd stated that one of the robbers was armed.

   1.____

2. A. Mr. Brown fired three shots from his revolver.
   B. Mr. Brown was shot in the head by one of the robbers.
   C. Mr. Brown suffered a gunshot wound of the head during the course of the robbery.
   D. Mr. Brown was taken to General Hospital by ambulance.

   2.____

3. A. Shots were fired after one of the robbers said, *Give us the money or we'll kill you.*
   B. After one of the robbers demanded the money from Mr. Brown, he fired a shot.
   C. The preliminary investigation indicated that although Mr. Brown did not have a license for the gun, he was justified in using deadly physical force.
   D. Mr. Brown was interviewed at General Hospital.

   3.____

4. A. Each of the witnesses were customers in the store at the time of occurrence.
   B. Neither of the witnesses interviewed was the owner of the liquor store.
   C. Neither of the witnesses interviewed were the owner of the store.
   D. Neither of the witnesses was employed by Mr. Brown.

   4.____

5. A. Mr. Brown arrived at General Hospital at about 5:00 P.M.
   B. Neither of the robbers was injured during the robbery.
   C. The robbery occurred at 3:30 P.M. on February 10.
   D. One of the witnesses called the ambulance.

   5.____

Questions 6-10.

DIRECTIONS: Each of Questions 6 through 10 consists of information given in outline form and four sentences labeled A, B, C, and D. For each question, choose the one sentence which CORRECTLY expresses the information given in outline form and which also displays PROPER English usage.

6. Client's Name: Joanna Jones
   Number of Children: 3
   Client's Income: None
   Client's Marital Status: Single

   A. Joanna Jones is an unmarried client with three children who have no income.
   B. Joanna Jones, who is single and has no income, a client she has three children.
   C. Joanna Jones, whose three children are clients, is single and has no income.
   D. Joanna Jones, who has three children, is an unmarried client with no income.

   6.____

7. Client's Name: Bertha Smith
Number of Children: 2
Client's Rent: $1050 per month
Number of Rooms: 4

7.____

    A. Bertha Smith, a client, pays $1050 per month for her four rooms with two children.
    B. Client Bertha Smith has two children and pays $1050 per month for four rooms.
    C. Client Bertha Smith is paying $1050 per month for two children with four rooms.
    D. For four rooms and two children client Bertha Smith pays $1050 per month.

8. Name of Employee: Cynthia Dawes
Number of Cases Assigned: 9
Date Cases were Assigned: 12/16
Number of Assigned Cases Completed: 8

8.____

    A. On December 16, employee Cynthia Dawes was assigned nine cases; she has completed eight of these cases.
    B. Cynthia Dawes, employee on December 16, assigned nine cases, completed eight.
    C. Being employed on December 16, Cynthia Dawes completed eight of nine assigned cases.
    D. Employee Cynthia Dawes, she was assigned nine cases and completed eight, on December 16.

9. Place of Audit: Broadway Center
Names of Auditors: Paul Cahn, Raymond Perez
Date of Audit: 11/20
Number of Cases Audited: 41

9.____

    A. On November 20, at the Broadway Center 41 cases was audited by auditors Paul Cahn and Raymond Perez.
    B. Auditors Raymond Perez and Paul Cahn has audited 41 cases at the Broadway Center on November 20.
    C. At the Broadway Center, on November 20, auditors Paul Cahn and Raymond Perez audited 41 cases.
    D. Auditors Paul Cahn and Raymond Perez at the Broadway Center, on November 20, is auditing 41 cases.

10. Name of Client: Barbra Levine
Client's Monthly Income: $2100
Client's Monthly Expenses: $4520

10.____

    A. Barbra Levine is a client, her monthly income is $2100 and her monthly expenses is $4520.
    B. Barbra Levine's monthly income is $2100 and she is a client, with whose monthly expenses are $4520.

C. Barbra Levine is a client whose monthly income is $2100 and whose monthly expenses are $4520.
D. Barbra Levine, a client, is with a monthly income which is $2100 and monthly expenses which are $4520.

Questions 11-13.

DIRECTIONS: Questions 11 through 13 involve several statements of fact presented in a very simple way. These statements of fact are followed by 4 choices which attempt to incorporate all of the facts into one logical statement which is properly constructed and grammatically correct.

11. I. Mr. Brown was sweeping the sidewalk in front of his house.
    II. He was sweeping it because it was dirty.
    III. He swept the refuse into the street.
    IV. Police Officer gave him a ticket.

    Which one of the following BEST presents the information given above?
    A. Because his sidewalk was dirty, Mr. Brown received a ticket from Officer Green when he swept the refuse into the street.
    B. Police Officer Green gave Mr. Brown a ticket because his sidewalk was dirty and he swept the refuse into the street.
    C. Police Officer Green gave Mr. Brown a ticket for sweeping refuse into the street because his sidewalk was dirty.
    D. Mr. Brown, who was sweeping refuse from his dirty sidewalk into the street, was given a ticket by Police Officer Green.

12. I. Sergeant Smith radioed for help.
    II. The sergeant did so because the crowd was getting larger.
    III. It was 10:00 A.M. when he made his call.
    IV. Sergeant Smith was not in uniform at the time of occurrence.

    Which one of the following BEST presents the information given above?
    A. Sergeant Smith, although not on duty at the time, radioed for help at 10 o'clock because the crowd was getting uglier.
    B. Although not in uniform, Sergeant Smith called for help at 10:00 A.M. because the crowd was getting uglier.
    C. Sergeant Smith radioed for help at 10:00 A.M. because the crowd was getting larger.
    D. Although he was not in uniform, Sergeant Smith radioed for help at 10:00 A.M. because the crowd was getting larger.

13. I. The payroll office is open on Fridays.
    II. Paychecks are distributed from 9:00 A.M. to 12 Noon.
    III. The office is open on Fridays because that's the only day the payroll staff is available.
    IV. It is open for the specified hours in order to permit employees to cash checks at the bank during lunch hour.

The choice below which MOST clearly and accurately presents the above idea is:
- A. Because the payroll office is open on Fridays from 9:00 A.M. to 12 Noon, employees can cash their checks when the payroll staff is available.
- B. Because the payroll staff is only available on Fridays until noon, employees can cash their checks during their lunch hour.
- C. Because the payroll staff is available only on Fridays, the office is open from 9:00 A.M. to 12 Noon to allow employees to cash their checks.
- D. Because of payroll staff availability, the payroll office is open on Fridays. It is open from 9:00 A.M. to 12 Noon so that distributed paychecks can be cashed at the bank while employees are on their lunch hour.

Questions 14-16.

DIRECTIONS: In each of Questions 14 through 6, the four sentences are from a paragraph in a report. They are not in the right order. Which of the following arrangements is the BEST one?

14. I. An executive may answer a letter by writing his reply on the face of the letter itself instead of having a return letter typed.
    II. This procedure is efficient because it saves the executive's time, the typist's time, and saves office file space.
    III. Copying machines are used in small offices as well as large offices to save time and money in making brief replies to business letters.
    IV. A copy is made on a copy machine to go into the company files, while the original is mailed back to the sender.

    The CORRECT answer is:
    A. I, II, IV, III   B. I, IV, II, III   C. III, I, IV, II   D. III, IV, II, I

14.____

15. I. Most organizations favor one of the types but always include the others to a lesser degree.
    II. However, we can detect a definite trend toward greater use of symbolic control.
    III. We suggest that our local police agencies are today primarily utilizing material control.
    IV. Control can be classified into three types: physical, material, and symbolic.

    The CORRECT answer is:
    A. IV, II, III, I   B. II, I, IV, III   C. III, IV, II, I   D. IV, I, III, II

15.____

16. I. They can and do take advantage of ancient political and geographical boundaries, which often give them sanctuary from effective policy activity.
    II. This country is essentially a country of small police forces, each operating independently within the limits of its jurisdiction.
    III. The boundaries that define and limit police operations do not hinder the movement of criminals, of course.
    IV. The machinery of law enforcement in America is fragmented, complicated, and frequently overlapping.

16.____

The CORRECT answer is:
A. III, I, IV B. II, IV, I, III C. IV, II, III, I D. IV, III, II, I

17. Examine the following sentence, and then choose from below the words which should be inserted in the blank spaces to produce the best sentence.
The unit has exceeded _____ goals and the employees are satisfied with _____ accomplishments.
A. their, it's B. it's; it's C. its, there D. its, their

17._____

18. Examine the following sentence, and then choose from below the words which should be inserted in the blank spaces to produce the best sentence.
Research indicates that employees who _____ no opportunity for close social relationships often find their work unsatisfying, and this _____ of satisfaction often reflects itself in low production.
A. have; lack B. have; excess C. has; lack D. has; excess

18._____

19. Words in a sentence must be arranged properly to make sure that the intended meaning of the sentence is clear.
The sentence below that does NOT make sense because a clause has been separated from the word on which its meaning depends is:
A. To be a good writer, clarity is necessary.
B. To be a good writer, you must write clearly.
C. You must write clearly to be a good writer.
D. Clarity is necessary to good writing.

19._____

Questions 20-21.

DIRECTIONS: Each of Questions 20 and 21 consists of a statement which contains a word (one of those underlined) that is either incorrectly used because it is not in keeping with the meaning the quotation is evidently intended to convey, or is misspelled. There is only one INCORRECT word in each quotation. Of the four underlined words, determine if the first one should be replaced by the word lettered A, the second one replaced by the word lettered B, the third one replaced by the word lettered C, or the fourth one replaced by the word lettered D.

20. The alleged killer was occasionally permitted to excercise in the corridor.
A. alledged B. ocasionally C. permited D. exercise

20._____

21. Defense counsel stated, in affect, that their conduct was permissible under the First Amendment.
A. council B. effect C. there D. permissable

21._____

Question 22.

DIRECTIONS: Question 22 consists of one sentence. This sentence contains an incorrectly used word. First, decide which is the incorrectly used word. Then, from among the options given, decide which word, when substituted for the incorrectly used word, makes the meaning of the sentence clear.

22. As today's violence has no single cause, so its causes have no single scheme. 22.____
    A. deference B. cure C. flaw D. relevance

23. In the sentence, *A man in a light-grey suit waited thirty-five minutes in the ante-room for the all-important document*, the word IMPROPERLY hyphenated is 23.____
    A. light-grey
    B. thirty-five
    C. ante-room
    D. all-important

24. In the sentence, *The candidate wants to file his application for preference before it is too late*, the word *before* is used as a(n) 24.____
    A. preposition
    B. subordinating conjunction
    C. pronoun
    D. adverb

25. In the sentence, *The perpetrators ran from the scene*, the word *from* is a 25.____
    A. preposition B. pronoun C. verb D. conjunction

KEY (CORRECT ANSWERS)

1.	D	11.	D
2.	D	12.	D
3.	A	13.	D
4.	B	14.	C
5.	D	15.	D
6.	D	16.	C
7.	B	17.	D
8.	A	18.	A
9.	C	19.	A
10.	C	20.	D

21. B
22. B
23. C
24. B
25. A

PREPARING WRITTEN MATERIAL

PARAGRAPH REARRANGEMENT
COMMENTARY

The sentences that follow are in scrambled order. You are to rearrange them in proper order and indicate the letter choice containing the correct answer at the space at the right.

Each group of sentences in this section is actually a paragraph presented in scrambled order. Each sentence in the group has a place in that paragraph; no sentence is to be left out. You are to read each group of sentences and decide upon the best order in which to put the sentences so as to form a well-organized paragraph.

The questions in this section measure the ability to solve a problem when all the facts relevant to its solution are not given.

More specifically, certain positions of responsibility and authority require the employee to discover connection between events sometimes, apparently, unrelated. In order to do this, the employee will find it necessary to correctly infer that unspecified events have probably occurred or are likely to occur. This ability becomes especially important when action must be taken on incomplete information.

Accordingly, these questions require competitors to choose among several suggested alternatives, each of which presents a different sequential arrangement of the events. Competitors must choose the MOST logical of the suggested sequences.

In order to do so, they may be required to draw on general knowledge to infer missing concepts or events that are essential to sequencing the given events. Competitors should be careful to infer only what is essential to the sequence. The plausibility of the wrong alternatives will always require the inclusion of unlikely events or of additional chains of events which are NOT essential to sequencing the given events.

It's very important to remember that you are looking for the best of the four possible choices, and that the best choice of all may not even be one of the answers you're given to choose from.

There is no one right way to solve these problems. Many people have found it helpful to first write out the order of the sentences, as they would have arranged them, on their scrap paper before looking at the possible answers. If their optimum answer is there, this can save them some time. If it isn't, this method can still give insight into solving the problem. Others find it most helpful to just go through each of the possible choices, contrasting each as they go along. You should use whatever method feels comfortable and works for you.

While most of these types of questions are not that difficult, we've added a higher percentage of the difficult type, just to give you more practice. Usually there are only one or two questions on this section that contain such subtle distinctions that you're unable to answer confidently. And you then may find yourself stuck deciding between two possible choices, neither of which you're sure about.

EXAMINATION SECTION

TEST 1

DIRECTIONS: Each question consists of several sentences which can be arranged in a logical sequence. For each question, select the choice which places the numbered sentences in the MOST logical sequence. *PRINT THE LETTER OF THE CORRECT ANSWER IN THE SPACE AT THE RIGHT.*

1.
   I. A body was found in the woods.
   II. A man proclaimed innocence.
   III. The owner of a gun was located.
   IV. A gun was traced.
   V. The owner of a gun was questioned.
   The CORRECT answer is:
   A. IV, III, V, II, I
   B. II, I, IV, III, V
   C. I, IV, III, V, II
   D. I, III, V, II, IV
   E. I, II, IV, III, V

   1.____

2.
   I. A man is in a hunting accident.
   II. A man fell down a flight of steps.
   III. A man lost his vision in one eye,
   IV. A man broke his leg.
   V. A man had to walk with a cane.
   The CORRECT answer is:
   A. II, IV, V, I, III
   B. IV, V, I, III, II
   C. III, I, IV, V, II
   D. I, III, V, II, IV
   E. I, III, II, IV, V

   2.____

3.
   I. A man is offered a new job.
   II. A woman is offered a new job.
   III. A man works as a waiter.
   IV. A woman works as a waitress.
   V. A woman gives notice.
   The CORRECT answer is:
   A. IV, II, V, III, I
   B. IV, II, V, I, III
   C. II, IV, V, III, I
   D. III, I, IV, II, V
   E. IV, III, II, V, I

   3.____

4.
   I. A train let the station late.
   II. A man was late for work.
   III. A man lost his job.
   IV. Many people complained because the train was late.
   V. There was a traffic jam.
   The CORRECT answer is:
   A. V, II, I, IV, III
   B. V, I, IV, II, III
   C. V, I, II, IV, III
   D. I, V, IV, II, III
   E. II, I, IV, V, III

   4.____

5. I. The burden of proof as to each issue is determined before trial and remains upon the same party throughout the trial.
    II. The jury is at liberty to believe one witness' testimony as against a number of contradictory witnesses.
    III. In a civil case, the party bearing the burden of proof is required to prove his contention by a fair preponderance of the evidence.
    IV. However, it must be noted that a fair preponderance of evidence does not necessarily mean a greater number of witnesses.
    V. The burden of proof is the burden which rests upon one of the parties to an action to persuade the trier of the facts, generally the jury, that a proposition he asserts is true.
    VI. If the evidence is equally balanced, or if it leaves the jury in such doubt as to be unable to decide the controversy either way, judgment must be given against the party upon whom the burden of proof rests.
    The CORRECT answer is:
    A. III. II, V, IV, I, VI B. I, II, VI, V, III, IV C. III, IV, V, I, II, VI
    D. V, I, III, VI, IV, II E. I, V, III, VI, IV, II

6. I. If a parent is without assets and is unemployed, he cannot be convicted of the crime of non-support of a child.
    II. The term *sufficient ability* has been held to mean sufficient financial ability.
    III. It does not matter if his unemployment is by choice or unavoidable circumstances.
    IV. If he fails to take any steps at all, he may be liable to prosecution for endangering the welfare of a child.
    V. Under the penal law, a parent is responsible for the support of his minor child only if the parent is of *sufficient ability*.
    VI. An indigent parent may meet his obligation by borrowing money or by seeking aid under the provisions of the Social Welfare Law.
    The CORRECT answer is:
    A. VI, I, V, III, II, IV B. I, III, V, II, IV, VI C. V, II, I, III, VI, IV
    D. I, VI, IV, V, II, III E. II, V, I, III, VI, IV

7. I. Consider, for example, the case of a rabble rouser who urges a group of twenty people to go out and break the windows of a nearby factory.
    II. Therefore, the law fills the indicated gap with the crime of *inciting to riot*.
    III. A person is considered guilty of inciting to riot when he urges ten or more persons to engage in tumultuous and violent conduct of a kind likely to create public alarm.
    IV. However, if he has not obtained the cooperation of at least four people, he cannot be charged with unlawful assembly.
    V. The charge of inciting to riot was added to the law to cover types of conduct which cannot be classified as either the crime of *riot* or the crime of *unlawful assembly*.
    VI. If he acquires the acquiescence of at least four of them, he is guilty of unlawful assembly even if the project does not materialize.
    The CORRECT answer is:
    A. III, V, I, VI, IV, II B. V, I, IV, VI, II, III C. III, IV, I, V, II, VI
    D. V, I, IV, VI, III, II E. V, III, I, VI, IV, II

8. I. If, however, the rebuttal evidence presents an issue of credibility, it is for the jury to determine whether the presumption has, in fact, been destroyed.
    II. Once sufficient evidence to the contrary is introduced, the presumption disappears from the trial.
    III. The effect of a presumption is to place the burden upon the adversary to come forward with evidence to rebut the presumption.
    IV. When a presumption is overcome and ceases to exist in the case, the fact or facts which gave rise to the presumption still remain.
    V. Whether a presumption has been overcome is ordinarily a question for the court.
    VI. Such information may furnish a basis for a logical inference.
    The CORRECT answer is:
    A. IV, VI, II, V, I, III
    B. III, II, V, I, IV, VI
    C. V, III, VI, IV, II, I
    D. V, IV, I, II, VI, III
    E. II, III, V, I, IV, VI

9. I. An executive may answer a letter by writing his reply on the face of the letter itself instead of having a return letter typed.
    II. This procedure is efficient because it saves the executive's time, the typist's time, and saves office file space.
    III. Copying machines are used in small offices as well as large offices to save time and money in making brief replies to business letters.
    IV. A copy is made on a copying machine to go into the company files, while the original is mailed back to the sender.
    The CORRECT answer is:
    A. I, II, IV, III
    B. I, IV, II, III
    C. III, I, IV, II
    D. III, IV, II, I

10. I. Most organizations favor one of the types but always include the others to a lesser degree.
    II. However, we can detect a definite trend toward greater use of symbolic control.
    III. We suggest that our local police agencies are today primarily utilizing material control.
    IV. Control can be classified into three types: physical, material, and symbolic.
    The CORRECT answer is:
    A. IV, II, III, I
    B. II, I, IV, III
    C. III, IV, II, I
    D. IV, I, III, II

11. I. Project residents had first claim to this use, followed by surrounding neighborhood children.
    II. By contrast, recreation space within the project's interior was found to be used more often by both groups.
    III. Studies of the use of project grounds in many cities showed grounds left open for public use were neglected and unused, both by residents and by members of the surrounding community.
    IV. Project residents had clearly laid claim to the play spaces, setting up and enforcing unwritten rules for use.
    V. Each group, by experience, found their activities easily disrupted by other groups, and their claim to the use of space for recreation difficult to enforce.

The CORRECT answer is:
A. IV, V, I, II, III
B. V, II, IV, III, I
C. I, IV, III, II, V
D. III, V, II, IV, I

12. I. They do not consider the problems correctable within the existing subsidy formula and social policy of accepting all eligible applicants regardless of social behavior.
II. A recent survey, however, indicated that tenants believe these problems correctable by local housing authorities and management within the existing financial formula.
III. Many of the problems and complaints concerning public housing management and design have created resentment between the tenant and the landlord.
IV. This same survey indicated that administrators and managers do not agree with the tenants.
The CORRECT answer is:
A. II, I, III, IV
B. I, III, IV, II
C. III, II, IV, I
D. IV, II, I, III

12.____

13. I. In single-family residences, there is usually enough distance between tenants to prevent occupants from annoying one another.
II. For example, a certain small percentage of tenant families has one or more members addicted to alcohol.
III. While managers believe in the right of individuals to live as they choose, the manager becomes concerned when the pattern of living jeopardizes others' rights.
IV. Still others turn night into day, staging lusty entertainments which carry on into the hours when most tenants are trying to sleep.
V. In apartment buildings, however, tenants live so closely together that any misbehavior can result in unpleasant living conditions.
VI. Other families engage in violent argument.
The CORRECT answer is:
A. III, II, V, IV, VI, I
B. I, V, II, VI, IV, III
C. II, V, IV, I, III, VI
D. IV, II, V, VI, III, I

13.____

14. I. Congress made the commitment explicit in the Housing Act of 194, establishing as a national goal the realization of a *decent home and suitable environment for every American family.*
II. The result has been that the goal of decent home and suitable environment is still as far distant as ever for the disadvantaged urban family.
III. In spite of this action by Congress, federal housing programs have continued to be fragmented and grossly underfunded.
IV. The passage of the National Housing Act signaled a few federal commitment to provide housing for the nation's citizens.
The CORRECT answer is:
A. I, IV, III, II
B. IV, I, III, II
C. IV, I, II, III
D. II, IV, I, III

14.____

15.
I. The greater expense does not necessarily involve *exploitation*, but it is often perceived as exploitative and unfair by those who are aware of the price differences involved, but unaware of operating costs.
II. Ghetto residents believe they are *exploited* by local merchants, and evidence substantiates some of these beliefs.
III. However, stores in low-income areas were more likely to be small independents, which could not achieve the economies available to supermarket chains and were, therefore, more likely to charge higher prices, and the customers were more likely to buy smaller-sized packages which are more expensive per unit of measure.
IV. A study conducted in one city showed that distinctly higher prices were charged for goods sold in ghetto stores in other areas.

The CORRECT answer is:
A. IV, II, I, III   B. IV, I, III, II   C. II, IV, III, I   D. II, III, IV, I

15.____

KEY (CORRECT ANSWERS)

1.	C	6.	C	11.	D
2.	E	7.	A	12.	C
3.	B	8.	B	13.	B
4.	B	9.	C	14.	B
5.	D	10.	D	15.	C

EXAMINATION SECTION
TEST 1

DIRECTIONS: The sentences that follow are in scrambled order. You are to rearrange them in proper order and indicate the letter choice containing the CORRECT answer. *PRINT THE LETTER OF THE CORRECT ANSWER IN THE SPACE AT THE RIGHT.*

1. Fire Marshal Adams has arrested a man for pulling a false alarm. He has recorded the following items of information about the incident in his notebook for use in his subsequent report:
    I. I was on surveillance at a frequently pulled false alarm box located at Edison Street and Harvard Road.
    II. At 1605 hours, I observed the white male, with long brown hair and a mustache, wearing black pants and a red shirt, pull the fire alarm box.
    III. I interviewed the officer of the first due ladder company, Lt. Morgan - L-37, who informed me that a search of the area disclosed no cause for an alarm to be transmitted.
    IV. A man wearing a red shirt, black pants, with long brown hair and a mustache came out of Ryan's Pub, located at Edison Street and Harvard Road, and walked directly to the alarm box.
    V. I stopped the man about five blocks away at 33rd Street and Harvard Road and asked him why he pulled the fire alarm box, and he replied, *Because I felt like it.*

    The MOST logical order for the above sentences to appear in the report is

    A. I, IV, II, III, V
    B. I, II, III, IV, V
    C. I, IV, III, II, V
    D. I, IV, V, II, III

1.____

2. A fire marshal is preparing a report regarding Tom Jones, who was a witness to an arson fire at his apartment building. Following are five sentences which will be included in the report:
    I. On July 16, I responded to the fire building, address 2020 Elm Street, to interview Tom Jones.
    II. Tom Jones described the *super* (name unknown) as a middle-aged male with beard, six feet tall, wearing a blue jumpsuit.
    III. Tom Jones stated that he saw the *super* of the building next door set the fire.
    IV. After being advised of his constitutional rights at the 44th Precinct detective's squad room, the *super* confessed.
    V. I interviewed the *super* and took him to the precinct for further investigation.

    The MOST logical order for the above sentences to appear in the report is

    A. I, II, III, V, IV
    B. I, II, III, IV, V
    C. I, III, II, IV, V
    D. I, III, II, V, IV

2.____

135

3. A fire marshal is preparing a report on a shooting incident which will include the following five sentences:
   I. I ran around the corner and observed a man pointing a gun at another man.
   II. I informed the man I was a police officer and that he should drop his gun.
   III. I was on the corner of 4th Avenue and 43rd Street when I heard a gunshot coming from around the corner.
   IV. The man turned around and pointed his gun at me.
   V. I fired once, shooting him in the chest and causing him to fall to the ground.
   The MOST logical order for the above sentences to appear in the report is

   A. I, III, IV, II, V   B. IV, V, II, I, III
   C. III, I, II, IV, V   D. III, I, V, II, IV

4. Fire Marshal Smith is writing a report. The report will include the following five sentences:
   I. I asked the woman for a description of the man and his location in the building.
   II. When I said, *Don't move, Five Marshal,* the man dropped the can containing a flammable liquid.
   III. I transmitted on my handie-talkie for fire companies to respond.
   IV. A woman approached our car and said there was a man pouring a liquid, which she thought to be gasoline, on a staircase at 123 East Street.
   V. Upon entering that location, I observed a man spilling a liquid on the floor.
   The MOST logical order for the above sentences to appear on the interview sheet is

   A. IV, I, V, II, III   B. I, IV, III, V, II
   C. V, II, IV, I, III   D. IV, III, I, V, II

5. Fire Marshal Fox is completing an interview report for a fire in the kitchen of an apartment at 1700 Clayton Road. The following five sentences will be included in the interview report:
   I. This is the first fire in which Mrs. Brown has ever been involved.
   II. A neighbor smelled the food burning and called the Fire Department.
   III. Mrs. Brown has been a tenant in Apt. 4C for 7 years.
   IV. Mrs. Brown was very tired and laid down to rest and fell asleep.
   V. Mrs. Brown was cooking beef stew in the kitchen after coming home from work.
   The MOST logical order for the above sentences to appear in the report is

   A. II, III, I, IV, V   B. III, V, IV, II, I
   C. I, III, II, V, IV   D. III, V, I, IV, II

6. A fire marshal is completing a report of an arson fire. The report will contain the following five statements made by a witness:
   I. I heard the sound of breaking glass; and when I looked out my window, I saw orange flames coming from the building across the street.
   II. I saw two young men on bicycles rapidly riding away, one with long blond hair, the other had long brown hair.
   III. He made a threat to get even when he was being evicted.
   IV. The young man with long blond hair was evicted from the fire building last week.
   V. The two young men rode in the direction of Flowers Avenue.
   The MOST logical order for the above statements to appear in the report is

A. I, II, V, IV, III   B. I, II, IV, V, III
C. III, I, V, II, IV   D. III, I, II, IV, V

7. A fire marshal is preparing a report regarding an eleven-year-old who was burned in a fire at the Midtown School for Boys. The report will include the following five sentences:
    I. The child described the fire-setter as a male with glasses, five feet tall, wearing a blue uniform.
    II. On December 12, I responded to Hill Top Hospital to interview a child who was burned in a fire at the Midtown School for Boys.
    III. The male perpetrator made a full confession in front of the Assistant District Attorney at the precinct.
    IV. I responded to the school, after interviewing the boy, and found a security guard who fit the description.
    V. I interviewed the security guard and took him to the precinct for further questioning.
   The MOST logical order for the above sentences to appear in the fire report is

   A. I, IV, V, II, III   B. IV, III, II, I, V
   C. II, I, IV, V, III   D. II, IV, I, V, III

8. A fire marshal is preparing a report concerning a fire in an auto body shop. The report will contain the following five sentences:
    I. The shop owner stated that he argued with a customer about the cost of a repair job.
    II. The shop owner will be the complainant in the arson case.
    III. While on surveillance, my partner and I saw the fire and called it in over the Department radio.
    IV. The customer paid the bill and left saying, *I'll fix you for charging so much.*
    V. According to witnesses, the customer returned to the shop and threw a Molotov cocktail on the floor.
   The MOST logical order for the above sentences to appear in the report is

   A. I, IV, V, II, III   B. III, I, IV, V, II
   C. V, I, IV, III, II   D. III, V, I, IV, II

9. Security Officer Mace is completing an entry in her memo-book. The entry has the following five sentences:
    I. I observed the defendant removing a radio from a facility vehicle.
    II. I placed the defendant under arrest and escorted him to the patrolroom.
    III. I was patrolling the facility parking lot.
    IV. I asked the defendant to show identification. V. I determined that the defendant was not authorized to remove the radio.
   The MOST logical order for these sentences to be entered in Officer Mace's memo-book is

   A. I, III, II, IV, V   B. II, V, IV, I, III
   C. III, I, IV, V, II   D. IV, V, II, I, III

10. Security Officer Riley is completing an entry in his memo-book. The entry has the following five sentences:
    I. Anna Jones admitted that she stole Mary Green's wallet.
    II. I approached the women and asked them who they were and why they were arguing.
    III. I arrested Anna Jones for stealing Mary Green's wallet.
    IV. They identified themselves and Mary Green accused Anna Jones of stealing her wallet.
    V. I was in the lobby area when I observed two women arguing about a wallet.
    The MOST logical order for these sentences to be entered in Officer Riley's memo-book is

    A. II, IV, I, III, V
    B. III, I, IV, V, II
    C. IV, I, V, II, III
    D. V, II, IV, I, III

11. Assume that Security Officer John Ryan is completing an entry in his memobook. The entry has the following five sentences:
    I. I then cleared the immediate area of visitors and staff.
    II. I noticed smoke coming from a broom closet outside Room A71.
    III. Sergeant Mueller arrived with other officers to assist in clearing the area.
    IV. Upon investigation, I determined the smoke was due to burning material in the broom closet.
    V. I pulled the corridor fire alarm and notified Sergeant Mueller of the fire.
    The MOST logical order for these sentences to be entered in Officer Ryan's memo-book is

    A. II, III, IV, V, I
    B. II, IV, V, I, III
    C. IV, I, II, III, V
    D. V, III, II, I, IV

12. Security Officer Hernandez is completing an entry in his memobook. The entry has the following five sentences:
    I. I asked him to leave the premises immediately.
    II. A visitor complained that there was a strange man loitering in Clinic B hallway.
    III. I went to investigate and saw a man dressed in rags sitting on the floor of the hallway.
    IV. As he walked out, he started yelling that he had no place to go.
    V. I asked to see identification, but he said that he did not have any.
    The MOST logical order for these sentences to be entered in Officer Hernandez's memobook is

    A. II, III, V, I, IV
    B. III, I, II, IV, V
    C. IV, I, V, II, III
    D. III, I, V, II, IV

13. Officer Hogan is completing an entry in his memobook. The entry has the following five sentences:
    I. When the fighting had stopped, I transmitted a message requesting medical assistance for Mr. Perkins.
    II. Special Officer Manning assisted me in stopping the fight,
    III. When I arrived at the scene, I saw a client, Adam Finley, strike a facility employee, Peter Perkins.
    IV. As I attempted to break up the fight, Special Officer Manning came on the scene.
    V. I received a radio message from Sergeant Valez to investigate a possible fight in progress in the waiting room.

    The MOST logical order for these sentences to be entered in Officer Hogan's memobook is

    A. II, I, IV, V, III
    B. III, V, II, IV, I
    C. IV, V, III, I, II
    D. V, III, IV, II, I

14. Police Officer White is preparing a crime report concerning the burglary of Mr. Smith's home. The report will contain the following five sentences:
    I. Upon entering the house, Mr. Smith noticed that the mortgage money, which had been left on the kitchen table, had been taken.
    II. An investigation by the reporting Officer determined that the burglar had left the house through the first floor rear door.
    III. Further investigation revealed that there were no witnesses to the burglary.
    IV. In addition, several pieces of jewelry were missing from a first floor bedroom.
    V. After arriving at home, Mr. Smith discovered that someone had broken into the house by jimmying the front door.

    The MOST logical order for the above sentences to appear in the report is

    A. V, IV, II, III, I
    B. V, I, III, IV, II
    C. V, I, IV, II, III
    D. V, IV, II, I, III

15. Police Officer Jenner responds to the scene of a burglary at 2106 La Vista Boulevard. He is approached by an elderly man named Richard Jenkins, whose account of the incident includes the following five sentences:
    I. I saw that the lock on my apartment door had been smashed and the door was open.
    II. My apartment was a shambles; my belongings were everywhere and my television set was missing.
    III. As I walked down the hallway toward the bedroom, I heard someone opening a window.
    IV. I left work at 5:30 P.M. and took the bus home.
    V. At that time, I called the police.

    The MOST logical order for the above sentences to appear in the report is

    A. I, V, IV, II, III
    B. IV, I, II, III, V
    C. I, V, II, III, IV
    D. IV, III, II, V, I

16. Police Officer LaJolla is writing an Incident Report in which back-up assistance was required. The report will contain the following five sentences:
    I. The radio dispatcher asked what my location was and he then dispatched patrol cars for back-up assistance.
    II. At approximately 9:30 P.M., while I was walking my assigned footpost, a gunman fired three shots at me.
    III. I quickly turned around and saw a White male, approximately 5'10", with black hair, wearing blue jeans, a yellow T-shirt, and white sneakers, running across the avenue carrying a handgun.
    IV. When the back-up officers arrived, we searched the area but could not find the suspect.
    V. I advised the radio dispatcher that a gunman had just fired a gun at me, and then I gave the dispatcher a description of the man.

    The MOST logical order for the above sentences to appear in the report is

    A. III, V, II, IV, I
    B. II, III, V, I, IV
    C. III, II, IV, I, V
    D. II, V, I, III, IV

17. Police Officer Engle is completing a Complaint Report of a burglary which occurred at Monty's Bar. The following five sentences will be included in the Complaint Report:
    I. The owner said that approximately $600 was taken, along with eight bottles of expensive brandy.
    II. The burglar apparently gained entry to the bar through the window and exited through the front door.
    III. When Mr. Barrett returned to reopen the bar at 1:00 P.M., he found the front door open and items thrown all over the bar.
    IV. Mr. Barrett, the owner of Monty's Bar, said he closed the bar at 4:00 M. and locked all the doors.
    V. After interviewing the owner, I conducted a search of the bar and found that a window in the back of the bar was broken.

    The MOST logical order for the above sentences to appear in the report is

    A. II, IV, III, V, I
    B. IV, III, I, V, II
    C. IV, II, III, I, V
    D. II, V, IV, III, I

18. Police Officer Revson is writing a report concerning a vehicle pursuit. His report will include the following five sentences:
    I. I followed the vehicle for several blocks and then motioned to the driver to pull the car over to the curb and stop.
    II. I informed the radio dispatcher that I was in a high-speed pursuit.
    III. When the driver ignored me, I turned on my siren and the driver increased his speed.
    IV. The vehicle hit a tree, and I was able to arrest the driver.
    V. While on patrol in Car #4135, I observed a motorist driving suspiciously.

    The MOST logical order for the above sentences to appear in the report is

    A. V, I, III, II, IV
    B. II, V, III, I, IV
    C. V, I, II, IV, III
    D. II, I, V, IV, III

19. Crime Reports are completed by Police Officers. One section of a report contains the following five sentences:
    I. The man, seeing that the woman had the watch, pushed Mr. Lugano to the ground.
    II. Frank Lugano was walking into the Flame Diner on Queens Boulevard when he was jostled by a man in front of him.
    III. A few minutes later, Mr. Lugano told a police officer on foot patrol about a man and a woman taking his watch.
    IV. As soon as he was jostled, a woman reached toward Mr. Lugano's wrist and removed his expensive watch.
    V. The man and woman, after taking Mr. Lugano's watch, ran around the corner.

    The MOST logical order for the above sentences to appear in the report is

    A. II, IV, I, III, V
    B. II, IV, I, V, III
    C. IV, I, III, II, V
    D. IV, II, I, V, III

20. Detective Adams completed a Crime Report which includes the following five sentences:
    I. I arrived at the scene of the crime at 10:20 A.M. and began to question Mr. Sands about the security devices he had installed.
    II. Several clearly identifiable fingerprints were found.
    III. A Fingerprint Unit specialist arrived at the scene and immediately began to dust for fingerprints.
    IV. After questioning Mr. Sands, I called the Fingerprint Unit.
    V. On Friday morning at 10 A.M., Mr. Sands, the owner of the High Fashion Fur Store on Fifth Avenue, called the precinct to report that his safe had been broken into.

    The MOST logical order for the above sentences to appear in the Crime Report is

    A. I, V, IV, III, II
    B. I, V, III, IV, II
    C. V, I, IV, II, III
    D. V, I, IV, III, II

KEY (CORRECT ANSWERS)

1.	A	11.	B
2.	D	12.	A
3.	C	13.	D
4.	A	14.	C
5.	B	15.	B
6.	A	16.	B
7.	C	17.	B
8.	B	18.	A
9.	C	19.	B
10.	D	20.	D

TEST 2

DIRECTIONS: The sentences that follow are in scrambled order. You are to rearrange them in proper order and indicate the letter choice containing the CORRECT answer. *PRINT THE LETTER OF THE CORRECT ANSWER IN THE SPACE AT THE RIGHT.*

1. Police Officer Ling is preparing a Complaint Report of a missing person. His report will contain the following five sentences:
    I. I was greeted by Mrs.Miah Ali, who stated her daughter Lisa, age 17, did not return from school.
    II. I questioned Mrs. Ali as to what time her daughter left for school and what type of clothing she was wearing.
    III. I notified the Patrol Sergeant, searched the building and area, and prepared a Missing Person Complaint Report.
    IV. I received a call from the radio dispatcher to respond to 9 Maple Street, Apartment 1H, on a missing person complaint.
    V. Mrs. Ali informed me that Lisa was wearing a grey suit and black shoes, and departed for school at 7:30 A.M.
   The MOST logical order for the above sentences to appear in the report is

   A. IV, I, V, II, III
   B. I, IV, V, III, II
   C. IV, I, II, V, III
   D. III, I, IV, II, V

   1.____

2. Police Officer Dunn is preparing a Complaint Report which will include the following five sentences:
    I. Mrs. Field screamed and fought with the man.
    II. A man wearing a blue ski mask grabbed Mrs. Field's purse.
    III. Mrs. Field was shopping on 34th Street and Broadway at 1 o'clock in the afternoon.
    IV. The man then ran around the corner.
    V. The man was white, five feet six inches tall with a medium build.
   The MOST logical order for the above sentences to appear in the report is

   A. I, V, II, IV, III
   B. III, II, I, IV, V
   C. III, IV, V, I, II
   D. V, IV, III, I, II

   2.____

3. Police Officer Davis is preparing a written report concerning child abuse. The report will include the following five sentences:
    I. I responded to the scene and was met by an adult and a child who was approximately four years old.
    II. I was notified by an unidentified pedestrian of a possible case of child abuse at 325 Belair Terrace.
    III. The adult told me that the child fell and that the police were not needed.
    IV. I felt that this might be a case of child abuse, and I requested that a Sergeant respond to the scene.
    V. The child was bleeding from the head and had several bruises on the face.
   The MOST logical order for the above sentences to appear in the report is

   A. II, I, V, III, IV
   B. I, II, IV, III, V
   C. I, III, IV, II, V
   D. II, IV, I, V, III

   3.____

142

2 (#2)

4. The following five sentences will be part of a memobook entry concerning found property:

    I. Mr. Gustav said that while cleaning the lobby he found six credit cards and a passport.
    II. The credit cards and passport were issued to Manuel Gomez.
    III. I went to the precinct to give the property to the Desk Officer.
    IV. I prepared a receipt listing the property, gave the receipt to Mr. Gustav, and had him sign my memobook.
    V. While on foot patrol, I was approached by Mr. Gustav, the superintendent of 50-12 Maiden Parkway.

The MOST logical order for the above sentences to appear in the memobook is

A. V, I, II, IV, III
B. I, II, IV, III, V
C. V, I, III, IV, II
D. I, IV, III, II, V

5. Police Officer Thomas is making a memobook entry that will include the following five sentences:

    I. My partner obtained a brief description of the suspects and the direction they were heading when they left the store.
    II. Edward Lemkin was asked to come with us to search the immediate area.
    III. I transmitted this information over the radio.
    IV. At the corner of 72nd Street and Broadway, our patrol car was stopped by Edward Lemkin, the owner of PJ Records.
    V. He told us that a group of teenagers stole some merchandise from his record store.

The MOST logical order for the above sentences to appear in the report is

A. V, IV, I, III, II
B. IV, V, I, III, II
C. V, I, III, II, IV
D. IV, I, III, II, V

6. Police Officer Caldwell is completing a Complaint Report. The report will include the following five sentences:

    I. When I yelled, *Don't move, Police,* the taller man dropped the bat and ran.
    II. I asked the girl for a description of the two men.
    III. I called for an ambulance.
    IV. A young girl approached me and stated that a man with a baseball bat was beating another man in front of 1700 Grande Street.
    V. Upon approaching the location, I observed the taller man hitting the other man with the bat.

The MOST logical order for the above sentences to appear in the report is

A. IV, V, I, II, III
B. V, IV, II, III, I
C. V, I, III, IV, II
D. IV, II, V, I, III

7. Police Officer Moore is writing a memobook entry concerning a summons he issued. The entry will contain the following five sentences:
   I. As I was walking down the platform, I heard music coming from a radio that a man was holding on his shoulder.
   II. I asked the man for some identification.
   III. I was walking in the subway when a passenger complained about a man playing a radio loudly at the opposite end of the station.
   IV. I then gave the man a summons for playing the radio. V. As soon as the man saw me approaching, he turned the radio off.
   The MOST logical order for the above sentences to appear in the memobook entry is

   A. III, V, II, I, IV
   B. I, II, V, IV, III
   C. III, I, V, II, IV
   D. I, V, II, IV, III

8. Police Officer Kashawahara is completing an Incident Report regarding fleeing suspects he had pursued earlier. The report will include the following five sentences:
   I. I saw two males attempting to break into a store through the front window.
   II. On Myrtle Avenue, they ran into an alley between two abandoned buildings.
   III. I yelled to them, *Hey, what are you guys doing by that window?*
   IV. At that time, I lost sight of the suspects and I returned to the station house.
   V. They started to run south on Wycoff Avenue heading towards Myrtle Avenue.
   The MOST logical order for the above sentences to appear in the report is

   A. I, V, II, IV, III
   B. III, V, II, IV, I
   C. I, III, V, II, IV
   D. III, I, V, II, IV

9. Police Officer Bloom is completing an entry in his memo-book regarding a confession made by a perpetrator. The entry will include the following five sentences:
   I. I went towards the dresser and took $400 in cash and a jewelry box with rings, watches, and other items in it.
   II. There in the bedroom, lying on the bed, a woman was sleeping.
   III. It was about 1:00 A.M. when I entered the apartment through an opened rear window.
   IV. I spun around, punched her in the face with my free hand, and then jumped out the window into the street.
   V. I walked back to the window carrying the money and the jewelry box and was about to go out when all of a sudden I heard the woman scream.
   The MOST logical order for the above sentences to appear in the memobook entry is

   A. I, III, II, V, IV
   B. I, V, IV, III, II
   C. III, II, I, V, IV
   D. III, V, IV, I, II

10. Police Officer Webster is preparing an Arrest Report which will include the following five sentences:
    I. I noticed that the robber had a knife placed at the victim's neck.
    II. I told the robber to drop the knife.
    III. While on patrol, I observed a robbery which was in progress.
    IV. I grabbed the robber, placed him in handcuffs, and took him to the precinct.
    V. The robber dropped the knife and tried to flee.
    The MOST logical order for the above sentences to appear in the report is

    A. I, II, V, IV, III
    B. III, I, II, V, IV
    C. III, II, IV, I, V
    D. I, III, IV, V, II

11. Police Officer Lee is preparing a report regarding someone who apparently attempted to commit suicide with a gun. The report will include the following five sentences:
    I. At the location, the woman pointed to the open door of Apartment 7L.
    II. I called for an ambulance to respond.
    III. The male had a gun in his hand and a large head wound.
    IV. A call was received from the radio dispatcher regarding a woman who heard a gunshot at 936 45th Avenue.
    V. Upon entering Apartment 7L, I saw the body of a male on the kitchen floor.

    The MOST logical order for the above sentences to appear in the report is

    A. IV, I, V, III, II
    B. I, III, V, IV, II
    C. I, V, III, II, IV
    D. IV, V, III, II, I

12. Police Officer Modrak is completing a memobook entry which will include the following five sentences:
    I. The victim, a male in his thirties, told me that the robbery occurred a few minutes ago.
    II. My partner and I jumped out of the patrol car and arrested the suspect.
    III. We responded to an armed robbery in progress at Billings Avenue and 59th Street.
    IV. On Chester Avenue and 68th Street, the victim spotted and identified the suspect.
    V. I told the victim to get into the patrol car and that we would drive him around the area.

    The MOST logical order for the above sentences to appear in the memobook is

    A. III, I, V, IV, II
    B. I, III, V, II, IV
    C. I, IV, III, V, II
    D. III, V, I, II, IV

13. Police Officer Rodriguez is preparing a report concerning an incident in which she used her revolver. Her report will include the following five sentences:
    I. Upon seeing my revolver, the robber dropped his gun to the ground.
    II. At about 10:55 P.M., I was informed by a passerby that several people were being robbed at gunpoint on 174th Street and Walton Avenue.
    III. I was assigned to patrol on 174th Street and Ghent Avenue during the evening shift.
    IV. I saw a man holding a gun on three people, took out my revolver, and shouted, Police, don't move!
    V. After calling for assistance, I went to 174th Street and Walton Avenue and took cover behind a car.

    The MOST logical order for the above sentences to appear in the report is

    A. II, III, IV, V, I
    B. IV, V, I, III, II
    C. III, II, V, IV, I
    D. II, IV, I, V, III

14. Police Officer Davis is completing an Activity Log entry which will include the following five sentences:

    I. A radio car was dispatched and the male was taken to Greenville Hospital.
    II. Several people saw him and called the police.
    III. A naked man was running down the street waving his arms above his head and screaming, *Insects are all over me!*
    IV. I arrived on the scene and requested an ambulance.
    V. The dispatcher informed me that no ambulances were available.

    The MOST logical order for the above sentences to appear in the Activity Log is

    A. III, IV, V, I, II
    B. II, III, V, I, IV
    C. III, II, IV, V, I
    D. II, IV, III, V, I

15. Police Officer Peake is completing an entry in his Activity Log. The entry contains the following five sentences:

    I. He went to his parked car only to find he was blocked in.
    II. The owner of the vehicle refused to move the van until he had finished his lunch.
    III. Approximately 30 minutes later, I arrived on the scene and ordered the owner of the van to remove the vehicle.
    IV. Mr. O'Neil had an appointment and was in a hurry to keep it.
    V. Mr. O'Neil entered a nearby delicatessen and asked if anyone in there drove a dark blue van, license plate number BUS 265.

    The MOST logical order for the above sentences to appear in the Activity Log is

    A. II, III, I, IV, V
    B. IV, I, V, II, III
    C. V, IV, I, III, II
    D. II, I, III, IV, V

16. Police Officer Harrison is preparing a report regarding a 10-year-old who was sexually abused at school. The report will include the following five sentences:

    I. The child described the perpetrator as a white male with a mustache, six feet tall, wearing a green uniform.
    II. On September 10, I responded to General Hospital to interview a child who was sexually abused.
    III. He later confessed at the station house.
    IV. After I interviewed the child, I responded to the school and found a janitor who fit the description.
    V. I interviewed the janitor and took him to the station house for further investigation.

    The MOST logical order for the above sentences to appear in the report is

    A. II, IV, I, V, III
    B. I, IV, V, II, III
    C. II, I, IV, V, III
    D. V, III, II, I, IV

17. Police Officer Madden is completing a report of a theft. The report will include the following five sentences:
    I. I followed behind the suspect for two blocks.
    II. I saw a man pass by the radio car carrying a shopping bag.
    III. I looked back in the direction he had just come from and noticed that the top of a parking meter was missing.
    IV. As he saw me, he started to walk faster, and I noticed a red piece of metal with the word *violation* drop out of the shopping bag.
    V. When I saw a parking meter in the shopping bag, I apprehended the suspect and placed him under arrest.

    The MOST logical order for the above sentences to appear in the report is

    A. I, IV, II, III, V
    B. II, I, IV, V, III
    C. II, IV, III, I, V
    D. III, II, IV, I, V

18. Police Officer McCaslin is preparing a report of disorderly conduct which will include the following five sentences:
    I. Police Officer Kenny and I were on patrol in a radio car when we received a dispatch to go to the Hard Rock Disco on Third Avenue.
    II. We arrived at the scene and found three men arguing loudly and obviously intoxicated.
    III. The dispatcher had received a call from a bartender regarding a dispute.
    IV. Two of the men left the disco shortly before we did.
    V. We calmed the men down after managing to separate them.

    The MOST logical order for the above sentences to appear in the report is

    A. I, II, V, III, IV
    B. III, I, IV, II, V
    C. II, I, III, IV, V
    D. I, III, II, V, IV

19. Police Officer Langhorne is completing a report of a murder. The report will contain the following five statements made by a witness:
    I. The noise created by the roar of a motorcycle caused me to look out of my window.
    II. I ran out of the house and realized the man was dead, which is when I called the police.
    III. I saw a man driving at high speed down the dead-end street on a motorcycle, closely followed by a green BMW.
    IV. The motorcyclist then parked the bike and approached the car, which was occupied by two males.
    V. Two shots were fired and the cyclist fell to the ground; then the car made a u-turn and sped down the street.

    The MOST logical order for the above sentences to appear in the report is

    A. I, II, IV, III, V
    B. V, II, I, IV, III
    C. I, III, IV, V, II
    D. III, IV, I, II, V

20. Police Officer Murphy is preparing a report of a person who was assaulted. The report will include the following five sentences:
    I. I responded to the scene, but Mr. Jones had already fled.
    II. She was bleeding profusely from a cut above her right eye.
    III. Mr. and Mrs. Jones apparently were fighting in the street when Mr. Jones punched his wife in the face.
    IV. I then applied pressure to the cut to control the bleeding.
    V. I called the dispatcher on the radio to send an ambulance to respond to the scene.

    The MOST logical order for the above sentences to appear in the report is

    A. III, II, IV, I, V
    B. III, I, II, IV, V
    C. I, V, II, III, IV
    D. II, V, IV, III, I

KEY (CORRECT ANSWERS)

1.	C	11.	A
2.	B	12.	A
3.	A	13.	C
4.	A	14.	C
5.	B	15.	B
6.	D	16.	C
7.	C	17.	C
8.	C	18.	D
9.	C	19.	C
10.	B	20.	B

EXAMINATION SECTION
TEST 1

DIRECTIONS: Each question or incomplete statement is followed by several suggested answers or completions. Select the one the BEST answers the question or completes the statement. *PRINT THE LETTER OF THE CORRECT ANSWER IN THE SPACE AT THE RIGHT.*

1. The pivotal factor in determining whether an event is an "emergency" is typically 1.____

    A. the degree to which the event was unexpected
    B. whether the event requires supplemental efforts to save lives and protect property, public health and safety
    C. whether the event causes a loss of life
    D. the severity and magnitude of the damage caused by the event

2. Which of the following is an activity that is included within the authority of the Federal Emergency Management Agency (FEMA)? 2.____

    A. Physically rescuing disaster victims
    B. Establishing building standards and zoning regulations that will help mitigate the adverse effects of a disaster
    C. Providing mobile communications systems that open emergency lines when commercial networks are down
    D. Taking the lead role in recovery efforts after a disaster

3. Which of the following is NOT a member of the command staff under the incident command system? 3.____

    A. Information officer
    B. Information officer
    C. Logistics officer
    D. Safety officer

4. The Federal Response Plan generally performs each of the following functions, EXCEPT 4.____

    A. grouping types of federal assistance under twelve emergency support functions
    B. designating a primary agency and support agency for each emergency support function
    C. providing loans and grants to state and local governments
    D. explaining how the federal government mobilizes and supports state and local response efforts

5. Under the Federal Response Plan, FEMA is the lead agency for the emergency support functions (ESFs) of 5.____
    I. Resources Support
    II. Communications
    III. Information and Planning
    IV. Urban Search and Rescue

    A. I only
    B. II and III

149

C. III and IV
D. I, II, III and IV

Questions 6 through 10 refer to the following scenario:

A freak winter storm has stalled out over Summit County, dropping a record 25 inches of snow in a single night. More snow is forecast over the next 2 days, and the temperature is supposed to remain well below freezing for at least the next week or so.

All over the county, stranded motorists and residents without power have overwhelmed the 911 dispatch center. Although road crews have been activated, many of the drivers can't get to their trucks. Local and state emergency operations centers have been activated, and a local state of emergency has been declared. The incident commander has set up the command post at the police precinct house in the heart of the downtown in the county seat. The incident will require a large number and range of resources.

6. The incident commander will activate general staff positions that will each be led by a(n)   6.____

    A. branch supervisor
    B. staging area manager
    C. division supervisor
    D. section chief

7. Because this incident covers a large geographic area and is likely to continue for a period of time, the incident commander should probably establish a(n)   7.____

    A. base
    B. casualty collection point
    C. staging area
    D. camp

8. After several hours, the operations section activates several staging areas, divisions, branches, and groups. Under the ICS's principle of unity of command, which of these managers are likely to report directly to the incident commander?   8.____

    A. Only the operations section chief
    B. The operations section chief and the staging area managers
    C. Branch supervisors and division leaders
    D. Any of the above managers

9. The incident commander has requested that the state department of transportation send road-clearing equipment to help with the incident. The department's representative would communicate with the incident command staff's   9.____

    A. information officer
    B. planning section chief
    C. liaison officer
    D. facilities unit manager

3 (#1)

10. After several days, a worker at the ICP is told that his position will be demobilized at the conclusion of the current operational period. The worker should
    I. update all files and records
    II. complete all work in progress, unless otherwise directed
    III. return or otherwise transfer custody of all equipment that he has signed for
    IV. brief his relief or immediate supervisor on the status of all work, pending assignments, needs, and special situations

    A. I and II
    B. II only
    C. II, III and IV
    D. I, II, III and IV

11. As defined by disaster relief agencies, weapons of mass destruction (WMDs) include
    I. radiation or radioactivity
    II. diseases or organisms
    III. toxic or poisonous chemicals, or their precursors

    A. I only
    B. I and II
    C. II and III
    D. I, II and III

12. Without a presidential declaration of disaster, federal disaster assistance may include each of the following, EXCEPT

    A. firefighting assistance
    B. tax refunds
    C. unemployment insurance
    D. search and rescue

13. Typically, hazard analysis determines
    I. how hazards are likely to affect the community
    II. when the next disaster is most likely to occur
    III. how well the community will be able to respond to a disaster
    IV. the costs of risk

    A. I only
    B. I and II
    C. I, III and IV
    D. I, II, III and IV

14. Each of the following is a responsibility of an incident commander, EXCEPT

    A. managing assigned resources
    B. maintaining accountability
    C. coordinating the community-wide response
    D. protecting life and property

15. Federal mission assignments

    A. may be requested by counties and cities
    B. are usually issued to meet all eligible requests for federal assistance

C. can be issued before a disaster declaration
D. meet needs that exceed state and local government resources

16. The federal government's most important contribution to hazard mitigation efforts in any given community will likely be to

    A. ensure that all federal facilities in the community are built or retrofitted to reduce hazard vulnerability
    B. provide adequate funding for hazard mitigation
    C. take a leadership role in the planning stages of hazard mitigation activities
    D. controlling the costs of over-ambitious state and local mitigation programs

17. "Unity of command" in the incident command system refers to the fact that

    A. each member reports to only one supervisor
    B. each member reports to the incident commander
    C. all members share responsibility for decision-making in the operations function of incident response
    D. all members share responsibility for overall incident management

18. An emergency operations plan (EOP)
    I. assigns responsibility for mitigation concerns to local officials
    II. explains how people and property will be protected in emergencies
    III. identifies resources available for use during response and recovery operations
    IV. establishes lines of authority

    A. I and II
    B. II and III
    C. II, III and IV
    D. III and IV

19. What component of emergency management is defined as "sustained actions taken to reduce or eliminate the long-term risk to people and property from hazards and their effects?"

    A. Risk analysis
    B. Vulnerability assessment
    C. Preparedness
    D. Mitigation

20. Under federal regulations, all organizations that respond to _____ incidents are required to use the incident command system.
    I. flood
    II. fire
    III. hazardous materials
    IV. hurricane or tornado

    A. I only
    B. I, II and IV
    C. II and III
    D. III only

21. Which of the following is a federal program that funds state and local pre-disaster flood-plain planning and projects?

    A. Flood Mitigation Assistance
    B. 406
    C. Increased Cost of Compliance
    D. Hazard Mitigation Grant

22. The Community Rating System is an element of the National Flood Insurance Program that can
    I. decrease a community's flood insurance premiums
    II. provide an incentive for new flood mitigation, planning, and preparedness activities
    III. increase a community's flood insurance premiums
    IV. be made available to non-NFIP communities

    A. I only
    B. I and II
    C. I and III
    D. I, II, III and IV

23. At the scene of a major storm, an operations section chief understands that her span of control will be exceeded when the requested resources arrive. There is a need to assign resources geographically. One effective way to maintain her span of control would be to assign personnel to

    A. units
    B. divisions
    C. bases
    D. strike teams

24. The federal emergency public assistance program provides funds to

    A. businesses for economic recovery after a disaster
    B. individuals for temporary housing
    C. private nonprofit universities and colleges for mitigation research
    D. state and local governments for response and recovery activities

25. The federal cost share for _____ programs is 100%

    A. emergency work
    B. crisis counseling
    C. permanent, restorative work
    D. "other needs" assistance

KEY (CORRECT ANSWERS)

1.	B	11.	D
2.	C	12.	C
3.	C	13.	A
4.	C	14.	C
5.	C	15.	D
6.	D	16.	A
7.	A	17.	A
8.	A	18.	C
9.	C	19.	D
10.	D	20.	D

21. A
22. B
23. B
24. D
25. B

TEST 2

DIRECTIONS: Each question or incomplete statement is followed by several suggested answers or completions. Select the one the BEST answers the question or completes the statement. *PRINT THE LETTER OF THE CORRECT ANSWER IN THE SPACE AT THE RIGHT.*

1. An effective emergency management plan is characterized by
    I. overlapping command functions between jurisdictions
    II. modular organization
    III. separate police and fire command posts
    IV. common terminology

    A. I only
    B. I and III
    C. II and IV
    D. I, II, III and IV

    1.____

2. Emergency Management Mutual Aid (EMMA) is
    I. a means of establishing federal control over a disaster situation
    II. coordinated by FEMA
    III. a system for moving emergency management personnel to other jurisdictions that need assistance
    IV. a way of providing continuous 24-hour-a-day management during a disaster

    A. I only
    B. I and II
    C. III and IV
    D. I, II, III and IV

    2.____

3. A combination of personnel and equipment-such as a search and rescue team and an EMS team assigned to locate and treat several people trapped in the debris of a building collapse-is usually called a(n) _____ in the incident command system.

    A. division
    B. task force
    C. unit
    D. strike team

    3.____

4. In the Federal Response Plan, an Emergency Support Team (EST)

    A. responds to presidential disaster or emergency declarations
    B. coordinates multi-state and multi-regional operations
    C. deploys to high-visibility, catastrophic disasters
    D. coordinates early response operations with the state

    4.____

5. Disaster loans for homeowners, renters, business owners and nonprofit organizations are administered and funded by the

    A. Small Business Administration (SBA)
    B. Department of Housing and Urban Development (HUD)
    C. Federal Emergency Management Agency (FEMA)
    D. American Red Cross

    5.____

Questions 6 through 9 refer to the following scenario:

At around midnight, the 911 call center receives a call from the maintenance department of a local nursing home. Fire alarms have sounded in the west residential hall, which is a four-story win Smoke can be seen from the fourth floor. The hall houses 300 residents, and there are reports that some residents are trapped inside.

Fire Battalion 6 is immediately dispatched. After an initial assessment, the Battalion Chief requests a general alarm and assigns a safety officer, a liaison officer, and a full general staff.

6. The first priority of the planning section will be to

   A. develop response goals and objectives
   B. monitor safety conditions
   C. assess the resource needs of the situation
   D. contact other agencies assigned to the incident

7. In addition to the incident command post, the incident will require
   I. at least one staging area
   II. several bases
   III. a casualty collection point (CCP)
   IV. a camp

   A. I only
   B. I and III
   C. II, III and IV
   D. I, II, III and IV

8. A local counselor, a trauma expert, is asked to help calm arriving family members who fear their loved ones are trapped in the fire. Upon arriving at the scene, the counselor should check in with the _____ unit of the planning section.

   A. medical
   B. ground support
   C. facilities
   D. resources

9. Search and rescue teams are able to locate most, but not all, of the victims from the building. After some time, it becomes clear that these victims are dead. The incident commander has requested that several local churches, synagogues, and mosques help provide short-term shelter for the newly homeless victims of the fire. He has also requested the help of several local mental health professionals to assist the family members who are grieving for the dead. After representatives from these outside agencies check in, they should work with the

   A. liaison officer
   B. planning section chief
   C. logistics section chief
   D. safety officer

10. Which of the following is an activity that is NOT included within the authority of the Federal Emergency Management Agency (FEMA)?

    A. Administering the National Flood Insurance Program
    B. Providing "buy out" funding to relocate homes and businesses away from high-risk areas
    C. Creating risk assessment maps to aid local planners
    D. Operating temporary feeding stations or shelters after a disaster

11. Under the incident command system, which of the following has the authority to bypass the chain of command when necessary?

    A. Logistics officer
    B. Liaison officer
    C. Operations section chief
    D. Safety officer

12. Which of the following agencies provides AmeriCorps assistance following a disaster?

    A. Peace Corps
    B. Corporation for National Service (CNS)
    C. Department of Labor
    D. Department of Health and Human Services

13. A community that wants to participate in the National Flood Insurance Program must
    I. elevate roadbeds and homes that lie within a floodplain
    II. eliminate all known flood hazards
    III. adopt and enforce a floodplain management ordinance
    IV. conduct a flood hazard assessment

    A. I only
    B. II only
    C. III only
    D. III and IV

14. In federal mission assignment processing, which of the following typically occurs FIRST?

    A. the mission assignment is routed in the National Emergency Management Information System (NEMIS) for electronic signature
    B. the mission assignment coordinator or action tracker enters information from the action request form into the National Emergency Management Information System (NEMIS)
    C. funds are obligated in the financial system for mission assignment
    D. an operations section chief directs issuance of a mission assignment

15. Upon arrival at the scene of a disaster, the response team's FIRST action would most likely be to

    A. form initial opinions about the incident's requirements
    B. appoint a logistics officer
    C. develop an action plan
    D. establish a media liaison

16. The predicted impact that a hazard would have on people, services, facilities, and structures in a community is known specifically as

    A. vulnerability
    B. hazard identification
    C. risk
    D. incidence

17. A state that is considered a "Managing State" under FEMA's mitigtion programs
    I. contributes up to 80 percent of HMGP project costs
    II. has concluded a Memorandum of Understanding (MOU) with FEMA to perform specific Hazard Mitigation Grant Program project review functions
    III. reviews infrastructure projects for mitigation opportunities
    IV. can approve Hazard Mitigation Grant Program projects subject to environmental review.

    A. I and III
    B. II and IV
    C. II, III and IV
    D. I, II, III and IV

18. Which of the following is NOT a member of the general staff of an incident command system?

    A. Logistics officer
    B. Operations section chief
    C. Safety officer
    D. Incident commander

19. The lists of hazards developed during a hazard analysis will be compiled using
    I. community records
    II. historical data
    III. existing hazard analyses
    IV. computer simulations

    A. I and II
    B. I, II, and III
    C. III only
    D. I, II, III and IV

20. Which of the following is NEVER an allowable cost that can be submitted by states to federal disaster reimbursement programs?

    A. advertisements seeking temporary personnel for the disaster recovery efforts
    B. services of state building inspectors
    C. expenses incurred by the Officer of the Governor
    D. messenger/courier services

21. The STAPLE criteria are a means of determining the feasibility of _____ actions.

    A. mitigation
    B. preparation
    C. response
    D. recovery

22. An incident command system has been fully expanded to accommodate large-scale operations. In this case, the staging area manager would report to the

    A. operations section chief
    B. incident commander
    C. facilities unit leader
    D. logistics officer

22.____

23. At the state level, which of the following actions would occur at the "response" phase of disaster response?

    A. Issuing a disaster proclamation
    B. Requesting federal assistance
    C. Conducting mitigation efforts
    D. Activating and staffing an emergency operations center

23.____

24. The responsibility for identifying hazards and launching mitigation strategies typically belongs to

    A. the federal government
    B. state governments
    C. local governments
    D. businesses and individuals

24.____

25. FEMA's role in disaster assistance includes
    I. responding to requests from local governments
    II. managing the president's Disaster Relief Fund
    III. evaluating a state's request for a presidential declaration
    IV. advising the president on whether or not to make a declaration

    A. I and II
    B. III only
    C. II, III and IV
    D. I, II, III and IV

25.____

KEY (CORRECT ANSWERS)

1.	C	11.	D
2.	C	12.	B
3.	B	13.	C
4.	B	14.	D
5.	A	15.	A
6.	C	16.	C
7.	B	17.	B
8.	D	18.	D
9.	A	19.	B
10.	D	20.	C

21. A
22. A
23. B
24. C
25. C

EXAMINATION SECTION
TEST 1

DIRECTIONS: Each question or incomplete statement is followed by several suggested answers or completions. Select the one the BEST answers the question or completes the statement. *PRINT THE LETTER OF THE CORRECT ANSWER IN THE SPACE AT THE RIGHT.*

1. Typically, the primary responsibility for mitigation lies at the level of the 1.____

   A. state government
   B. individual citizens in a community
   C. federal government
   D. local government

2. Loss protection systems include 2.____
   - I. land use restrictions
   - II. seismic retrofitting
   - III. evacuation plans
   - IV. early-alert systems

   A. I and IV
   B. I, II and III
   C. I and III
   D. I, II, III and IV

3. At the scene of any emergency, the first priority of the incident commander is 3.____

   A. assessing incident priorities
   B. life safety
   C. stabilizing the incident
   D. coordinating overall emergency activities

4. Which of the authorities belongs exclusively to the federal government when an incident occurs? 4.____

   A. Coordinating federal, state, local and volunteer agencies
   B. Developing an Emergency Operations Plan
   C. Evacuating citizens
   D. Conducting preliminary damage assessments

5. Of the following, which type of federal assistance is provided EARLIEST during the emergency response process? 5.____

   A. SBA loans
   B. Insurance
   C. Cora Brown Fund
   D. Housing assistance

Questions 6 through 9 refer to the following scenario:

At a large resort hotel in a popular tourist port, a member of the kitchen staff spills a five-gallon bucket of caustic cleaner onto a hot griddle. The fumes immediately fill the kitchen, which is

2 (#1)

immediately evacuated, and enter the hotel's ventilation system. Within an hour, the hotel's front desk is receiving calls complaining of severe respiratory problems, nausea, vomiting, and severely irritated eyes, noses, and mouths. The hotel manager called the local 911 center immediately after the first call, and an ambulance and EMS team were sent to the scene. As many more guests reported their symptoms, additional medical teams were sent and the local hospital's emergency room was put on notice. Within two hours of the spill, more than 90 guests had re-quested hel More than 300 people are currently staying in the hotel.

Local resources are exhausted by the first two hours' emergency calls, and additional victims must be transported to other hospitals, some of which are more than 75 miles from the hotel. Helicopters will be needed for transport.

6. The incident commander will need to establish
   I. two bases
   II. at least one more incident command post
   III. a helibase
   IV. at least one staging area

   A. I and III
   B. II, III and IV
   C. III and IV
   D. I, II, III and IV

   6._____

7. The incident command system is fully expanded within the first three hours. The base manager will report to the

   A. planning section chief
   B. operations section chief
   C. situation unit leader
   D. facilities unit leader

   7._____

8. The incident commander receives hourly updates from the operations section chief on the status of resources. Resources at an incident will always be characterized as

   A. committed, unavailable, or at rest
   B. available or unavailable
   C. assigned, en route, or unavailable
   D. available, assigned, or out-of-service

   8._____

9. After the first few calls to the 911 center, the media are reporting rumors of a possible terror attack on the hotel. The incident commander should immediately establish a(n)

   A. communications center
   B. liaison officer
   C. press conference
   D. information officer

   9._____

10. Under the incident command system, which of the following is NOT a designated facility?

    A. Incident command post
    B. Casualty collection point
    C. Staging area
    D. Perimeter post

    10._____

11. In the federal emergency public assistance process, the specialist is responsible for

    A. conducting applicants' briefings
    B. designing large projects
    C. coordinating with the state government
    D. validating small projects

12. The most common natural disasters in the United States are

    A. earthquakes
    B. wildland fires
    C. tornadoes
    D. floods

13. Under the model of the incident command system, any function not assigned by the incident commander

    A. becomes the charge of the liaison officer
    B. is shared equally among battalion chiefs
    C. is the responsibility of the incident commander
    D. becomes the charge of the safety officer

14. At the state level, which of the following actions would occur at the "threat" or "impact" phase of disaster response?

    A. evaluating the need for federal assistance
    B. mobilizing resources
    C. beginning infrastructure support
    D. identifying staffing needs

15. The federal Hazard Mitigation Grant program offers federal assistance of up to _____ % of the cost of eligible post-disaster state and local mitigation measures.

    A. 25
    B. 49
    C. 75
    D. 100

16. Under the incident command system, resources are kept at the _____ while awaiting incident assignments.

    A. emergency operations center
    B. cache
    C. staging area
    D. incident command post

17. To clear roadways of debris in the aftermath of a major storm, the incident commander requests four Type 2 bulldozers. In this case, the resources have been classified

    A. by both type and kind
    B. by type
    C. by kind
    D. as single resources

18. Under federal mission assignments assistance, direct federal assistance 18.____

    A. is usually 100 percent federally funded
    B. supports federal responders
    C. is subject to cost share
    D. is requested by local governments

19. Of the following steps in preparing an "After-Action" report, which would be performed FIRST? 19.____

    A. Identifying unsolved problems
    B. Selecting issues that are focal points
    C. Developing recommendations on key issues for the main body of the report
    D. Identifying problems that have policy implications

20. In emergency management, the determination of a disaster's probability and impact is known specifically as 20.____

    A. risk assessment
    B. vulnerability analysis
    C. risk management
    D. risk analysis

21. Under the incident command system, a unit manager reports directly to the 21.____

    A. group supervisor
    B. branch supervisor
    C. logistics officer
    D. section chief

22. In the financial management of a disaster, "allocation" refers to 22.____

    A. the request and receipt of payments into a grantee's account
    B. setting aside funds for a specific program
    C. any payment to liquidate an obligation
    D. any formal reservation of funds

23. Which of the following is a structural solution to a flood hazard? 23.____

    A. Dam
    B. Levee
    C. Land use planning
    D. Wet floodproofing

24. Under the incident command system, the organizational level that has responsibility for a specified functional assignment at an incident is managed by a 24.____

    A. unit leader
    B. group supervisor
    C. section chief
    D. branch director

25. The main purpose of a Rapid Needs Assessment (RNA) at the state level is to
    A. determine the resources necessary to conduct life-saving and life-sustaining operations during the emergency response phase of a disaster
    B. provide voluntary agencies with information so they can assign the appropriate response staff
    C. gather information to support the governor's request for a presidential disaster declaration
    D. secure resources from unaffected areas of the state and disaster relief organizations

KEY (CORRECT ANSWERS)

1. D
2. D
3. B
4. A
5. B

6. C
7. D
8. D
9. D
10. D

11. D
12. D
13. C
14. A
15. C

16. C
17. A
18. C
19. A
20. D

21. B
22. B
23. B
24. B
25. A

TEST 2

DIRECTIONS: Each question or incomplete statement is followed by several suggested answers or completions. Select the one the BEST answers the question or completes the statement. *PRINT THE LETTER OF THE CORRECT ANSWER IN THE SPACE AT THE RIGHT.*

1. Which of the following is NOT associated with the response phase of emergency management?

    A. Debris removal
    B. Access control
    C. Mass care
    D. Rebuilding structures

2. In the midst of a major storm, a city bus has gone over an embankment and overturned on the edge of a wooded area. The required triage and treatment would BEST be performed at a(n)

    A. base
    B. staging area
    C. casualty collection point
    D. command and control point

3. In emergency management, the term "vulnerability analysis" is most accurately defined as

    A. the process of intervening to reduce risk
    B. the determination of the likelihood of an event occurring and the consequences of its occurrence
    C. a systematic method of determining the cost of risk
    D. the determination of the possible hazards that may cause harm

4. Under the model of the incident command system, an incident commander is responsible for
    I. evaluating plan effectiveness
    II. gathering and assigning resources
    III. communicating with other officials within the system
    IV. coordinating the overall incident response

    A. I and II
    B. II, III and IV
    C. III only
    D. I, II, III and IV

5. The mechanism by which FEMA provides funding to states to develop and maintain emergency management capabilities is the

    A. Performance Partnership Agreement (PPA)
    B. National Mitigation Strategy
    C. Emergency Management Mutual Aid (EMMA)
    D. Community Rating System

Questions 6 through 9 refer to the following scenario:

At around 10:30 on a weekday afternoon, a receptionist at Glenwood Federal Bank receives a call from a person claiming to have planted a bomb in the area of the bank. Because the bank manager could not immediately be located, the receptionist called the local police department to report the call and ask for help. Three patrol cars and a bomb disposal unit arrived at the bank within minutes of the receptionist's call.

6. The initial incident commander for this incident would be the　　　　　　　　　　　　　　6.____

    A. senior member of the bank staff
    B. receptionist
    C. senior member of the arriving police contingent
    D. bank manager

7. Which of the following tasks should be performed FIRST by the incident commander at the bank?　　　7.____

    A. Cordoning off the bank
    B. Setting up an information center
    C. Establishing command
    D. Evaluating the seriousness of the bomb threat

8. The incident commander should FIRST set up a(n)　　　　　　　　　　　　　　8.____

    A. media center
    B. incident command post (ICP)
    C. casualty collection point (CCP)
    D. staging area

9. After completing her initial assessment, the incident commander recognized a need for additional police officers. Under the incident command system, she would be requesting　　　9.____

    A. a division
    B. a task force
    C. single resources
    D. a strike force

10. Primary logistical functions for an incident are coordinated and administered at a(n)　　　10.____

    A. incident command post
    B. staging area
    C. base
    D. mobilization center

11. The president may deny a request for a disaster declaration if　　　　　　　　　　　　11.____
    I. the preliminary damage assessment is submitted on the incorrect forms
    II. the federal government determines that other sources can provide adequate assistance
    III. state and local governments are able to provide the necessary assistance
    IV. the federal legislature overturns the declaration

    A. I only
    B. II and III

C. II and IV
D. I, II, III and IV

12. A county's division of emergency management is seeking funds to retrofit its public buildings in order to make them more resistant to seismic activity. The county should apply for a _____ grant from the federal government

    A. disaster aid
    B. public assistance
    C. temporary disaster housing
    D. hazard mitigation

13. The incident command system designates the ideal number of subordinates to serve under a single supervisor during an incident as

    A. 3
    B. 5
    C. 8
    D. 12

14. In the financial management of a disaster at the federal level, which of the following would typically be performed LAST?

    A. The program office requests deobligation of excess funds not neede
    B. The allocation for the program is processed at FEMA headquarters
    C. A grantee draws down funds
    D. The program office prepares a worksheet to amend the initial allocation.

15. A community that wants to obtain aid for comprehensive mitigation planning should contact

    A. FEMA
    B. the state's NFIP liaison
    C. the state's hazard mitigation officer
    D. the state's office of emergency preparedness

16. Which element of an emergency team includes all twelve of the federally-defined emergency support functions (ESFs)?

    A. Logistics
    B. Mission Assignment
    C. Mobile Emergency Response System (MERS)
    D. Operations

17. In the financial management of a disaster, "drawdown" refers to the

    A. process of requesting and receiving payments into a grantee's account
    B. downward adjustment of a previously recorded obligation
    C. process of setting aside funds for a specific program
    D. formal reservation of funds

18. Which of the following is not a "disaster-dependent" program?

    A. Flood Mitigation Assistance Program
    B. Community Rating System
    C. Metropolitan Medical Response Service
    D. National Flood Insurance Program

19. Under the incident command system, three patrol units assigned to maintain crowd control would be defined as a

    A. strike team
    B. section
    C. division
    D. task force

20. Which of the following would be considered "permanent" work at a disaster site?

    A. Construction of a temporary bridge span over a flooding river or stream
    B. Installation of generators to provide power at public schools and hospitals
    C. Installation of seismic retrofits in older structures
    D. Debris clearance

21. _____ percent of public disaster assistance is assumed by the state(s) in which the disaster has occurred.

    A. 25
    B. 50
    C. 75
    D. 100

22. Ideally, the reconstruction of hazard-damaged structures should be accompanied by

    A. the adoption or augmentation of building codes to minimize risk
    B. strict land use controls
    C. greater percentage allowances for state and federal hazard mitigation funds to the structure's owner or owners
    D. increased insurance premiums

23. During the initial weeks of an emergency response, an "operational period" is typically _____ hours.

    A. 8
    B. 12
    C. 24
    D. 48

24. At the state level, the Governor's Authorized Representative

    A. interfaces with the Federal Coordinating Officer (FCO)
    B. executes all necessary documents on behalf of the State
    C. establishes a Disaster Field Office (DFO) and Disaster Recovery Centers (DRC)
    D. directs the activities of state departments and agencies

25. The incident command system requires written plans whenever
   I. resources from multiple agencies are used
   II. the incident involves hazardous materials
   III. the incident requires changes in personnel shifts or equipment
   IV. multiple jurisdictions are involved

   A. I and IV
   B. I, III and IV
   C. III and IV
   D. I, II, III and IV

KEY (CORRECT ANSWERS)

1. D
2. C
3. D
4. D
5. A

6. C
7. C
8. B
9. C
10. C

11. B
12. D
13. B
14. A
15. C

16. D
17. A
18. A
19. A
20. C

21. A
22. A
23. C
24. B
25. B

TRAINING PRINCIPLES AND PRACTICES

INTRODUCTION

1. Objective of Training — The WHY

   The purpose of training is to improve knowledge, skills, attitudes, and habits of employees so that they may better perform their assignments.

   Training needs can be defined on the basis of what the employee can do versus what he is required to do.

2. Time of Training Session — The WHEN

   Training needs can be identified from a study of existing records, such as turnover, absenteeism, grievances, production, waste of materials, number of *unsatisfactory* ratings, and accidents. Periodic surveys and interviews held with top level staff and line officials may locate areas in which training can help improve the operating services.

3. Space to be used to Conduct Session — The WHERE

   Availability of adequate space, free from noise and interruption; good ventilation and light.

4. Determine Teaching Method — The HOW

   a. Conference Technique. This is recognized as the most effective method for developing and improving proper work attitudes.
   b. Lecture Method. Use this method only where necessary information could not be obtained from the group.
   c. Role Play. Provides a learning experience by acting out situations found on the job.
   d. Field Trips Where Applicable.
   e. Case Studies. Review a case study as an aid in problem-solving.

5. Use of Training Aids — The WHAT

   a. Audiovisual
   b. Printed material, etc.

6. Use of Experts on Phases of Training — The WHO

   Good policy to select instructors from among the operating staff who have the capability and experience through training to assure effective presentation of subject matter.

Necessary Clearances from Top Management. Obtain management and employee support. A good relationship with all operating officials must prevail if they are to be encouraged to use the services that are available to them. Training staff to assist line must understand the special problems line is encountering.

Evaluate Program

Supervisors can check results by comparing past with present performance, attitudes and skills. Trainees opinions should be considered.

Did the Program accomplish its purpose?

LESSON PLAN — TRAINING

OBJECTIVES: The purpose of training is to improve skill, improve work habits, improve attitude and increase productivity.

It is the job of the supervisor to see that employees under his supervision are properly trained to do the job that is expected of them. The actual training may be done by the supervisor or may be delegated to a capable, experienced employee.

ADVANTAGES TO A SUPERVISOR OF HAVING A WELL-TRAINED STAFF

1. Gives supervisor time to devote to planning better supervision.
2. Permits supervisor time to train new and retrain old employees.
3. Promotes initiative.
4. Work can be carried on in absence of supervisor.
5. Increases prestige of supervisor in eyes of management.
6. Fewer accidents.
7. Employees have more confidence in themselves, resulting in higher morale.
8. Less damage to equipment.

PRINCIPLES OF LEARNING

1. Individuals must be receptive for maximum learning.
2. Individuals must be motivated and interested.
3. We learn by repetition.
4. We learn one thing at a time.
5. Instructions must be made simple and broken down to essentials.
6. We tie our new learning to what we already know.
7. Individual differences — We differ from one another in ability and background. We learn at different rates of speed.
8. Concentration and participation by employees are required for effective learning.
9. We learn better when there is continuity of thought — when one step logically follows another.
10. We learn better and faster when we realize we are making progress.
11. A competitive spirit speeds up learning.
12. The employee learns better when he has confidence in his ability to learn.
13. We learn through senses: What we know comes through the sense of:
    Sight - 75%; Hearing - 13%; Touch - 6%; Smell - 3%; Taste - 3%.
14. We must understand what we learn to use our learning effectivity.

FOUR-STEP APPROACH TO TRAINING

1. Preparation.
2. Presentation.
3. Try-out performance by learner.
4. Follow-up.
   a. Preparation: Considered from viewpoint of:
      (1) The instructor
      (2) The learner
      (3) The job
      (4) The facilities

      (a) The instructor - should prepare himself by deciding: The best way to do the job.
      The method to be used in instruction.
      The amount of instruction to give at each session.
      The teaching materials necessary and available.

      (b) The learner - should be prepared by: Being at ease.
      Finding out what he already knows about the job. Getting him interested in learning the job.

      (c) The job - should be analyzed completely, broken down to its component units, key points in each operation stressed.

      (d) The facilities - should be adequate and conducive to learning, such as:
      Adequate space, lighting, ventilation and visual aids. No distracting influences.

   b. Presentation:
      (1) Tell, show, illustrate and question carefully and patiently.
      (2) Stress key points
      (3) Illustrate clearly and completely, taking up one point at a time, but no more than he can master.

   c. Try-Out Performance by Learner. (Self-explanatory)

   d. Follow-up:
      (1) Put him on his own.
      (2) Designate to whom he goes for help.
      (3) Check frequently — encourage questions.
      (4) Get him to look for key points as he progresses.
      (5) Taper off extra coaching.

CONCLUSION: If the learner hasn't learned, the instructor hasn't taught.

SENSITIVITY TRAINING

The goal of *sensitivity training* is to make employees more sensitive to themselves and to others, to make them aware of how, consciously and unconsciously, they affect others and others influence them. A manager will do a better job of achieving results through the efforts of others if he has this heightened sensitivity to others. The sensitivity training situation is designed to bring to the surface, for conscious examination, the normally unquestioned assumptions regarding role behavior, spheres of authority and worker relationships. The characteristics of the sensitivity training situation include:

- No formal authority or status is recognized in the group.
- No agenda is established.
- No goal for the group to work toward is created.
- No prescribed way for the group to reach decisions is established.
- No instruction to participants is given by the instructor or *trainer*.
- Whatever the group wants to discuss is followed.

There are several disadvantages to sensitivity training. It is time-consuming, and often requires the group to live together for a period of time (usually 2 to 3 weeks). It may be unpleasant to certain individuals in the early stages of group discussions. However, almost all of the organizations that have used it have found it to be an effective method of promoting greater understanding of how groups operate and how individuals function in them.

SUPERVISOR'S CHECK LIST FOR ORIENTATION

1. Prepare to receive the new employee.

   a. Arrange for a private interview, if possible, if not it should at least be uninterrupted. Be prepared to give the new employee your undivided attention.
   b. Review his work experience, education and training.
   c. Have an up-to-date description of his job available for discussion.
   d. Have his work place, equipment and supplies ready.

2. Welcome the new employee.

   a. Welcome the new employee and call her by name.
   b. Indicate your relationship to the new employee.
   c. Make her feel wanted, that you consider her a valuable addition to your team; that her abilities and cooperation are needed to get the job done.
   d. Give her a feeling of confidence in herself. Tell her you have no doubt she will learn easily and that she will adjust readily to her new job.

3. Show genuine interest in the employee.

   a. Discuss his background and interests.
   b. Inquire about his transportation to and from work.

4. Explain facts about her job.

   a. Explain the specific functions of the unit.
   b. Explain her duties and responsibilities.
   c. Make clear what will be expected of her.
   d. Encourage her to ask questions.

- e. Show how her work is related to the work of others in the unit and how it fits into the work of the Department as a whole.
- f. Explain lines of authority.
- g. Explain to whom to go for help.

5. Sell the new employee on his job.

   a. Discuss with him the job advantages (friendly atmosphere, pleasant surroundings, security, promotion, pension, social security, municipal credit union, blood bank, grievance machinery and rewards for suggestions.)
   b. Sell him on his Department.
   c. Bring out the importance of his job in relation to the work of the unit and the Department as a whole.

6. Show employee the layout and facilities.

   a. Explain layout of unit or office.
   b. Show him facilities such as elevators, wash room, locker, etc.

7. Introduce him to co-workers.

   a. Indicate to each the new employee's duties.
   b. Explain duties of each person to whom introduced.
   c. Introduce to a well-qualified and trained sponsor who will go to lunch with the new employee and who will be available to answer questions.

8. Explain rules and regulations.

   a. Hours of work.
   b. Punctuality and attendance - signing in and out.
   c. Lunch period.
   d. Rest period.
   e. Use of telephone.
   f. Leave rules as administered.
   g. Other shop and office practices; smoking, safety regulations; safety program.
   h. Wearing of uniform, if required.
   i. Probationary period.
   j. Importance of good public relations.

9. Provide for job instruction

   Supervisor may instruct the new employee, or he may delegate this responsibility to a competent subordinate.

10. Follow-Up.

    a. Follow-up to see how new employee is progressing.
    b. Toward the end of the first day, show your personal interest by asking him how he is getting along or by encouraging him to ask questions, and by letting him know you want to be helpful.
    c. Make provision for frequent conferences with the new employee during the initial period of his employment.
    d. Keep the new employee posted on the progress he is making.

e. Continue to exercise close supervision with gradual tapering off as the employee demonstrates less need for close supervision.

SYSTEMS OF DIVIDING WORK AMONG EMPLOYEES

1. Series (or assembly-line)

   a. The assembly line approach, where each worker performs part of a job. For example, in an operation for collecting license fees, one employee checks the form, another collects the fees, and a third issues the receipt.
   b. Example - Sanitation, one worker loads, another drives truck.
   c. Advantages:
      (1) Short training for individual jobs which are relatively simple.
      (2) Greater availability of workers for simpler jobs when skilled labor market is tight.
      (3) Full use of highest skills of experienced employees on work requiring their skill.
   d. Disadvantages:
      (1) Added transportation and cycle time.
      (2) Reduced worker interest.
      (3) Added *comprehension* time.
      (4) Inflexibility of work force (inability to shift workers from one job to another to meet changing needs.)

2. Parallel

   a. A number of employees, each performing the complete job.
   b. Each worker checks form, collects fees, and issues receipt.
   c. Advantages:
      (1) Flexibility of work force.
      (2) Reduced comprehension time.
      (3) Reduced transportation of work item.
      (4) High worker interest.
   d. Disadvantages:
      (1) Increased training time.
      (2) Limited availability of higher skilled persons in employment market.
      (3) Use of some time of skilled workers on jobs not requiring highest skill.

3. Unit-assembly (simultaneous handling)

   a. Description - A number of operations are combined into a un:.t. Each worker on a team completes a different unit. Several teams are in operation.
   b. Advantages:
      (1) Same as those of serial plan.
      (2) Minimizes cycle-time.
   c. Disadvantages:
      (1) Same as those of serial plan, except for long cycle-time.
      (2) Can only be supplied in limited situations, where work 1 can be treated in separate parts.
      (3) Requires the addition of whatever steps are necessary to separate, route and reassemble work item.

4. Combination systems -- all possible combinations of serial, parallel and unit-assembly plans.

PROGRAM EVALUATION

Table of Contents

	Pages
Program Evaluation Strategy	1
Managing for Success	1
Types of Program Evaluation	1
Judging vs. Coaching	1
Conducting a Program Evaluation	3
The Need for Planning	3
Stage 1 - Evaluability Assessment	3
Performance Measurement	4
Mission, Goals and Objectives	4
Performance Indicators	5
Stage 2 - Designing the Evaluation	6
Stage 3 - Conducting the Study	8
Developing Data Measurement System	8
Determine Data Availability	9
Collecting Data	9
Analyzing Data	10
Data Presentation	10
Refining Measures	10
Stage 4 - Reporting Evaluation Findings	11
Stage 5 - Program Offices Implement Improvement Activities	12
Stage 6 - On-Going Consultation	13

PROGRAM EVALUATION

Program Evaluation Strategy

MANAGING FOR SUCCESS

An essential component of any successful organization is its ability to continually assess and evaluate its performance. To establish effective and efficient programs, managers need fundamental information regarding the position and progress of their programs, and what improvements can be made to enhance the overall quality of their operations.

In identifying this need, the PTO's Office of Planning and Evaluation (P&E) has developed an evaluation strategy for the Patent and Trademark Office. Our goal is to support PTO in planning, assessing, and improving its program activities, so that managers have the information and support they need to continually develop and advance their programs.

TYPES OF PROGRAM EVALUATION

Program evaluation is based on the fundamental idea that programs should have a demonstrable benefit.

In its simplest terms, program evaluation is defined as a systematic approach to assessing the performance of a program or service. Program evaluations are most commonly referred to as either summative or formative in nature. Summative evaluations make a judgment about a program's operations and usefulness, whereas formative evaluations describe a program's operations in order to improve the way in which it functions.

In recent years, the formative approach to evaluating has evolved into what has come to be called "evaluation research."

Evaluation research includes:
- Design of programs
- Ongoing monitoring of how well programs are functioning
- Assessment of program impact
- Analysis of benefits relative to costs.

This approach seems to be the most productive. As internal evaluators, our goal is not only to report to managers on their program's current situation, but also assist them in developing and enhancing the resources they need for continual operational improvement.

JUDGING VS. COACHING

In conducting formative evaluations, the goal is not to judge a program's worth or usefulness, rather the goal is to provide recommendations for program improvements in addition to assessing impacts and results.

A program evaluation trainer, uses the example of a world-class figure-skating champion to differentiate the roles of a coach and judge. As a skater performs, both the judge and the coach are meticulously assessing the skaters every move; however, each has a different motive for evaluating the performance. The judge looks at the performance and impassively scores the skater against the competition, providing little, if any, feedback to the skater. The coach on the other hand, goes a step beyond assessing the performance by actually working with the skater to improve his or her performance. The judge's objective is to score the skater's single performance, whereas the coach's objective is to help the skater achieve his or her fullest potential for future performances.

The coaching perspective helps programs become as efficient and effective as possible, while reaching their fullest potential. Using the example, the coach can work with and recommend improvements to the skater, but it is the skater who is responsible for making the improvements and for eventually becoming a guide and example for others that follow. By diagnosing, consulting and informing programs on their performance, we not only help programs gain a better understanding of what works well within their organization, we also maintain PTO's strategic goal of providing our customers with the highest level of quality and service in all aspects of PTO operations.

Conducting a Program Evaluation

In order to be effective, every evaluation must be tailored to the individual program or organization.

The following are stages in conducting a program evaluation. These stages are designed to adapt to individual needs, interests and the stage of development of the organization or program being evaluated.

THE NEED FOR PLANNING

Ideally, a successful evaluation will provide the best information possible on all key issues within a given set of constraints, such as available time, staff and budget resources. This makes it important to consider at the outset that the design of the evaluation needs to be done carefully, since criticism of the findings will likely focus on the methodology used.

Given the constraints we are all under these days, you may very well ask why you should spend precious resources on planning and designing your evaluation. The answer is precisely because of those constraints. In addition to increasing credibility in the product, a careful and sound design:

- increases overall quality,
- contains costs,
- ensures timeliness of findings,
- increases the strength and specificity of findings and recommendations,
- decreases criticism of methodology,
- improves customer satisfaction, and
- results in less resources required to carry out the evaluation.

STAGE 1: EVALUABILITY ASSESSMENT

Program evaluation is essentially a process in which questions are asked about a program or activity and answers are actively sought. In order to have an effective evaluation--which will result in improved program performance--first, the right questions must be asked, and second, the evaluation team must assure that the questions can be accurately answered.

Before conducting any formal evaluation, an evaluability assessment is conducted. The purpose of the evaluability assessment is to identify the program's goals, performance indicators and data sources, which will be used to conduct the evaluation. The evaluability assessment not only answers the question of whether a program can be meaningfully evaluated, but whether the evaluation is likely to contribute to improved program performance.

During the evaluability assessment there is usually a clear indication of whether a program is ready to be evaluated. If the necessary information (goals, objectives, performance measurements, etc.) is available and is identified by the evaluators and intended users as clear, concise and realistic (given resource allocations and restrictions), the evaluation can proceed. However, if the goals, objectives and performance indicators are found to be either underdeveloped or undefined, the program office is advised to first focus on developing or redefining their performance measurements before continuing with the evaluation.

The foremost question is whether or not the program can be evaluated in a meaningful way based on what currently exists.

Program evaluations are generally concerned with whether a program or policy is achieving its intended goal or purpose. Frequently though, the goals and purposes were to attract as much support as possible for the proposed project, but may lack consistency or be too ambitious given the realities of program functions. Programs and policies that do not have clear and consistent goals can not be evaluated for their effectiveness. Thus, uncovering those goals and purposes is generally the starting point of most evaluations. This first stage of an evaluation is necessary to determine whether they can be evaluated.

Program Evaluation Criteria

- Program goals and objectives, important side effects, and priority information needs are well defined.
- Program goals and objectives are plausible.
- Relevant performance data can be obtained.
- The intended users of the evaluation results have agreed on how they will use the information.

Performance Measurement

Performance measurement is a process by which a program objectively measures how it is accomplishing its mission through the delivery of its products, services, or processes. It is a self-assessment, goal-setting, and progress monitoring tool, which provides on-going performance feedback to both management and staff. A good performance measurement system is designed to provide information which helps clarify goals and motivates performance, solves problems, and corrects deviations or alters planned directions.

Performance Measurement is crucial to the overall management of programs because of one basic principle: "What gets measured, gets done."

Mission, Goals and Objectives

The first step in performance measurement is identifying the mission, goals and objectives. The following is a brief description of each:

The mission is the purpose for which a program or organization was created. A mission answers the following questions:

- Who are we?
- What do we do?
- For whom do we do it?
- Why do we do it?

Goals are statements, usually general and abstract, about how the program expects to accomplish its mission. Goals may be quantitative ("Increase production") or qualitative ("Improve worker morale").

> **Tips on Goal Setting**
>
> - Goals may be general or specific and may encompass time spans ranging from a few months to several years.
> - Goals may be set for the entire organization, programs, and individuals.
> - Goals at the various organizational levels must be coordinated if the organization is to achieve its intended overall purpose.
> - There must be coordination of the long-term goals of the organization with the short term goals of departments and programs, and of both of these with the personal goals of workers
> - Involve both management and staff when developing goals.

Objectives are the means for accomplishing goals. They must be quantifiable containing specific statements detailing the desired accomplishments of a program's goals.

> **Rules for Writing Objectives**
>
> - Use a single issue per objective.
>
> - Define measurable objectives using a verb-noun structure ("Increase productivity by 15 percent by fiscal year 2015").
>
> - Specify an expected time for achievement.

Performance Indicators

Once goals and objectives have been established, performance indicators are developed. Performance indicators track and measure whether the goals and objectives have been reached, or how well the program is progressing toward achieving them.

In the classical sense, a performance indicator is defined as a ratio where the output of an effort is divided by the inputs (labor, energy, time, etc.) required to produce it. . For example:

$$\frac{\text{\# of customers helped}}{\text{\# of service reps}}$$

$$\frac{\text{\# of acceptable documents produced}}{\text{hours expanded for documents}}$$

> **Customer Requirements and Stakeholder Requirements** are the Building Blocks for Measurement Ratios. When designing indicators ask the question: How Do We Know We Met Customer Requirements?

Two integral components of performance indicators are effectiveness and efficiency. Effective production is defined as producing the desired results, whereas efficient production is defined as producing the desired outputs with a minimum level of input. Simply stated, effectiveness is doing the right things, and efficiency is doing things right.

Effectiveness and efficiency are both critical measures of performance and success. Organizations can temporarily survive without perfect efficiency, but would most likely die if they were ineffective. When designing performance measurements, it is essential that an organization considers both effectiveness and efficiency. Omitting either would result in performance measurements that provide inaccurate and often costly productivity information.

It bears repeating that if a program has not clearly identified its goals and objectives and set effectiveness and efficiency measures, it will be difficult to evaluate.

Four Criteria for Measurement Effectiveness and Efficiency

1. **Quality-** The measure must define and reflect quality of production or services as well as quantity. A measure that assesses only quantity outputs can lead to reduced productivity.

2. **Mission and goals-** The measure must define and assess only outputs and services that are integrated with the organizational mission and strategic goals. Measures directed to products and services that are not consistent with mission and goals threaten productivity.

3. **Rewards and Incentives-** Measures must be integrated with performance incentives, reward systems and practices. Measures that have no important contingencies will not work to improve productivity.

4. **Employee Involvement-** There must be involvement of employees and other direct stakeholders in the definition and construction of productivity measures. When lack of involvement has not resulted in commitment and buy-in, results from the measures are not likely to be received favorably or to have any impact on future productivity.

STAGE 2: DESIGNING THE EVALUATION

What's worth knowing?
How will we get it?
How will it be used?

By the time you have an idea of the evaluation capacity of your program, you may have the answers to many of the questions that lead to the design. Every question asked by an evaluation can be looked at with varying levels of intensity and thoroughness. When great precision is needed and resources are available, the most powerful of evaluations may be conducted, on the other hand when time and resources are limited and only approximate answers are needed, the level of the evaluation will differ. Given the diversity of programs, policies and projects to be evaluated, the number of questions to be answered, and the differing availability of resources, there can be no single recipe for a successful evaluation. However, these simple guidelines, once tailored, should provide a solid framework for conducting an evaluation.

In determining the design of an evaluation, the following questions are answered and an Evaluation Design Proposal is drafted.

1. Why are we doing this evaluation?

Clarify what the overall purpose of the evaluation is and what specific objectives will be accomplished. Focus not only on what the evaluation will do, but also identify what the evaluation will NOT do.

2. For whom are we doing this evaluation?

It is essential to identify who the audience is so that their needs, perspectives and constraints can be assessed. Identify both the primary audience and secondary audiences.

Who is sponsoring the evaluation? Who is authorizing the expenditure of funds and human resources? Who will be approving the report?

3. What are we evaluating?

Discuss the issues of the evaluation. Are we studying the need for a program or activity? The operations of a program or activity? The effects of a program or activity? Define the specific questions to be answered during the evaluation.

4. How are we doing this evaluation?

Make a list of the information needed to conduct the evaluation. Once the information needs are defined, identify the data collection techniques. Examples of Data Collection Techniques:

- Surveys
- Interviews
- Focus Group Sessions
- Case Studies
- Tests
- Observations
- Document Reviews
- Production Reports
- Computerized databases

5. When are we doing this evaluation?

Establish both the beginning and completion dates and interim deadlines. It may be helpful to set up a project plan to track the dates and resources.

6. Where are we doing this evaluation?

Determine the location of the evaluation. Will a special staff be pulled together?
Will they need space for meetings? For working? For storage of files?

7. Who is doing this evaluation?

Assess the skills and resources needed to conduct the evaluation. Identify possible training needs and establish roles and responsibilities for each team member (Hendricks, 1994).

> **Tips on Building an Effective Study Team**
> - Keep teams small.
> - Acknowledge team members' need for high performance.
> - Reward both team leaders and team members.
> - Focus on people, not methodology.
> - Keep a skills inventory of team members.
> - Make use of project management tools to create benchmarks of success.
> - Form a policy group and a work group to involve policy makers, managers, and key staff in the evaluation.

Consider whether the skills and resources are available internally, or whether it might be more economical or beneficial to hire an external contractor to conduct the evaluation. Depending on the nature of the program or project, it may be critical that the results of the evaluation come from an outside, objective source.

One More Thing

After the design is completed, it is helpful to take an overall look at the design.

A well-designed evaluation can usually be recognized by the way it has:

1. Defined and posed questions for study.
2. Developed the methodological strategies for answering those questions.
3. Formulated a data collection plan that anticipates and addresses problems and obstacles that are likely to be encountered.
4. Provided a detailed analysis plan that will ensure that the questions posed will be answered with the appropriate data in the best possible fashion.
5. Established and maintained focus on the usefulness of the product for the intended user.

A sound design reduces downtime deciding what to do next, reduces time spent on collecting and analyzing irrelevant data and strengthens the relevance of the evaluation.

STAGE 3: CONDUCTING THE STUDY

Once the evaluation proposal is drafted and agreed upon by the evaluation team and the evaluation users, the process of collecting and analyzing the relevant data can begin.

DATA COLLECTION AND ANALYSIS

Developing A Data Measurement System

There are two methods of evaluation studies: qualitative and quantitative. Qualitative data collection systems permit the evaluator to study selected issues, cases, or events in depth and detail; data collection is not constrained by predetermined categories of analysis. Quantitative methods use standardized measures that fit diverse opinions and experiences into predetermined response categories. Considering evaluation design alternatives leads directly to consideration of the relative strengths and weaknesses of qualitative and quantitative studies, and the time and resources available for the study.

The advantage of the quantitative approach is that it measures the reactions of a great many people to a limited set of questions, thus facilitating comparison and statistical aggregation of the data. It gives a broad, generalized set of findings. Qualitative methods typically produce a wealth of detailed data about a much smaller number of people and cases. Qualitative data provide depth and detail through direct quotation and careful description of program situations, events, people, interactions, and observed behaviors.

Purposes and functions of qualitative and quantitative data are different, yet can be complementary. The statistics from standardized items make summaries, comparisons, and generalizations quite easy and precise. The narrative comments from open-ended questions are typically meant to provide a forum for elaboration, explanations, meanings, and new ideas.

It is recommended that an evaluation team engage stakeholders early because they have a different perspective, have data the evaluator needs, and can influence the evaluation positively if they are engaged, or negatively if they are ignored or threatened.

Categorizing research questions into major categories can help refine the research agenda of almost any study. Time spent in developing a detailed research design, data collection and analysis plan may improve the quality of the overall results.

Stakeholders include potential users of evaluation information and those with an investment in the organization or unit involved in the study.

Determine Data Availability

Once it has been established what to measure, it must be determined if the data for those measures is available and how to get it. If data is not available, alternative indicators must be identified.

The evaluation team should try to keep its indicators simple and use existing data whenever possible. However, do not compromise the evaluation by discarding indicators the team thinks are meaningful and important before weighing their obtainability.

Data Availability Concerns

1. Does the data currently exist ? If not, can it be developed, and at what effort and cost?
2. If the data exists, what will it cost to retrieve the data?
3. What will it take to get the data converted into the established measurement values?
4. Will a system investment be required? At what cost?
5. Will management support this level of cost? Can a limited version be used?
6. When will data be produced?

Collecting Data

The collection of data addresses the critical issues of making sure the correct data is identified, and a baseline is collected. The baseline data reflects the initial status of the program or process. During this phase, in addition to documenting the method of collection of the data, document any problems with the process, and work to resolve any process problems regularly. Meet with management at the end of an established trial period to evaluate results.

Analyzing Data

Once we have collected the data and before we meet with management, we must analyze the data to make sure that it will provide us with enough information and the right type of information on which to base an evaluation. We must ensure that the data fits the indicators identified to analyze. Agree to finalize the current indicators or revise them as needed, and analyze the baseline data collected for the purpose of setting goals.

DATA PRESENTATION

Once the data has been collected and analyzed, it must be decided how the data and results will be presented. Numbers by themselves are often difficult to understand, they cannot explain circumstances, and they may not easily lead to conclusions. Therefore, it is important to present the information in ways that make it easy to understand, that show relationships to other data, and that allow the information to be used to support decision-making processes. Whenever possible, use graphical tools to present data.

Measures must be shown in context. The most frequent evaluation contexts are: (1) goals compared to actual results, (2) trends in relation to previous periodic results, and (3) comparison of results to other relevant data. Using one or more of these contexts, meaningful conclusions should be drawn about the measurement result with little or no explanation.

REFINING MEASURES

Indicators may need some slight modifications or adjustment to better meet performance information needs of program or executive management. Continually check the usefulness of measurement data and adjust data collection methods if necessary.

Adjusting Measures

Are the measures working well?
What are the measures indicating?
Are additional indicators necessary?
Is data not really available (too difficult or expensive to acquire)?
Is data too difficult to use?

Balance Types Of Measures

One consideration of performance indicator development is that measures are interrelated and cannot be viewed in isolation. Timeliness, quality and cost are always in contention with each other, and the impact of improving any one or two must be weighed in relation to the expense of the third. A balance must be reached between the effectiveness and the economy and efficiency.

Consider Weighting Measures

Not all indicators are equally important. To reflect importance or priorities within measures or categories of measures, weight or index the measures. Weighting or indexing measures is an involved and advanced process and may not be necessary or appropriate for every program. However, weighting measures can provide some valuable insights into program outcomes.

Integrating with Management Process

Once performance results become available, the challenge shifts to presenting and using them effectively.

Establish Goals

Goals should be established based on: (1) policy or administrative priorities, (2) mission (3) customer feedback, (4) past history, (5) forecasted demand and (6) benchmark information.

Determine What The Measurements Say

It is extremely important to understand what the measurements say, as well as what they do not say. The measurements must be compared to performance goals, benchmarks, or past performance. Then variances or changes must be analyzed, and subsequent actions must be planned. In addition to program performance evaluation, the measurement results in the evaluation process can be used for external reporting, planning and budgeting activities and performance appraisal evaluation.

STAGE 4: REPORTING EVALUATION RESULTS

Reporting evaluation results is more of a process than a stage. Beginning on the first day of the evaluation, the evaluators should be continually reporting and discussing their findings with the evaluation users. It is not only important to keep them updated on the evaluation's progress, but also, it is important to keep them informed of any findings and recommendations that can be implemented before the full completion of the evaluation. Remember, the reason for doing an evaluation is to help an organization or program become as effective and efficient as possible. The sooner an organization can implement changes or improvements, the better.

Action-Oriented Reporting

As stated previously, the purpose of an evaluation is to improve a program or an organization's performance. The way in which evaluators do this is by providing recommendations for improvement to management and staff.

The majority of an evaluation report should be devoted to communicating the findings and specific recommendations. Reports should be action-oriented, centered mostly around the findings, but also around the recommendations and suggestions for implementation.

Action-oriented reports are often structured as a series of short reports targeted to specific audiences, rather than one all inclusive document.

Findings and recommendations should be presented clearly and concisely, in a way that meets the informational needs of the audience. In order for recommendations to be accepted by an organization, it must first understand what is being recommended and why it is relevant to their concerns. Evaluation studies are only useful if they are used.

Program Evaluation Report

Generally, an evaluation report should include:
- Executive Summary
  Purpose of Evaluation
  Program Background
  Evaluation Methodology
- Analysis of the Findings
- Recommendations

Tips for Reporting Evaluation Results

- Remember that the burden for effectively reporting results is on the evaluators, not the audience.

- Be aggressive. Instead of waiting for audiences to request information, actively look for opportunities to report results. Report regularly and frequently, appear in person if at all possible, and target multiple reports and briefings to specific audiences and /or issues.

- Simplify, simplify! Audiences are usually busy and their interest is pulled in different directions, so determine and report on the key points. If the core message creates interest, quickly follow up with more details.

- Study the audience. Learn about their backgrounds, interests, concerns, plans, pet peeves, etc.

- Focus on actions. Audiences are rarely interested in general information; they usually want guidance that will help them decide what to do next.

- Report in many different ways. Rather than using only one reporting technique or another, produce several different types of reports. Use written reports, personal briefings, screen show presentations, etc.

STAGE 5: PROGRAM OFFICES IMPLEMENT IMPROVEMENT ACTIVITIES

In this phase of the evaluation process, program office managers implement and monitor the recommendations and action plans originating from the evaluation study. The program manager facilitates the solution of problems by motivating staff and providing technical support. Particular attention must be given to customer and stakeholder requirements.

All employees should be trained in the process improvement recommendations so that they will possess the skills needed to recommend solutions to future problems. Decisions made closer to the customer and occurrence of events save time, reduce errors, and improve morale and service.

STAGE 6: ON-GOING CONSULTATION

Program evaluation is a continuous process of measuring, analyzing and refining an organization or program's performance.

A program evaluation is not an end in itself, rather it is the beginning of a continuous self-evaluation mechanism. With an effective evaluation comes additional data, refined measurements and new initiatives. In order to remain effective, organizations must continually evaluate this information to ensure the achievement of their mission, goals, and objectives.

www.ingramcontent.com/pod-product-compliance
Lightning Source LLC
Chambersburg PA
CBHW081813300426
44116CB00014B/2341